ENTERPRISE PERFORMANCE MANAGEMENT DONE RIGHT

ENTERPRISE PERFORMANCE MANAGEMENT DONE RIGHT

AN OPERATING SYSTEM FOR YOUR ORGANIZATION

Ron Dimon

WILEY

Library of Congress Cataloging-in-Publication Data:

ISBN 9781118370759 (Hardcover)
ISBN 9781118420669 (ebk)
ISBN 9781118434352 (ebk)
ISBN 9781118417133 (ebk)

Printed in the United States of America

10 9 8 7 6 5 4 3 2 1

For Harrison and Ruth - είστε πάντα στην καρδιά μου.

CONTENTS

FOREWORD

I have been involved with what is now called Enterprise Performance Management (EPM) in one way or another my entire career, whether it was in financial reporting and analysis or formulating strategy for our global business. I am a strong proponent of closing the gap between high-level strategy and day-to-day decisions, and of completing the cycle from a decision to its effectiveness. All too often we devise great plans and set out to execute them and then get overcome by events or sidetracked without coming back to see how relevant our plans were or how effective our decisions are.

Current economic demands and competitive pressure now require that we pay more attention to this cycle of Strategy, Plan, Execute, Analyze, and Improve. We must be more flexible and adaptable and be able to react to changing market conditions and customer preferences. And we must have a new level of accountability at all levels of our organizations. And with more mature and advanced EPM tools and the vast amounts of data at our disposal, there is no reason we should not be using this to give us more insight into the business and make faster, better decisions.

At Hyatt, we use our EPM capabilities to optimize all of our resources in pursuit of our goal of becoming the most preferred brand in each customer segment that we serve, not just for our guests but also for our managers, associates, and investors. The general managers at our full-service owned and managed hotels have an average tenure of more than 21 years at Hyatt. They are supported by regional management teams that use information, planning, analytics, and what-if modeling to support our general managers in achieving their goals. EPM is one of the foundational elements of our success and helps us focus on our mission of providing authentic hospitality.

EPM is not just another management fad or another technology buzzword. This is doing commonsense, fact-based management right. In this book, Ron Dimon shows us a way to think about EPM holistically and directly connects it to what's important in the business: sustainably delivering stakeholder value. The book provides a framework to hang your EPM roadmap onto, and helps you prioritize what's next on your journey to managing and improving performance. I wish you luck on that journey.

Gebhard Rainer, EVP and CFO
Hyatt Hotels Corporation
Chicago, IL
November 2012

PREFACE

Thank you for buying this book. It was a lot harder to write than I thought. The main problem was removing content—there is so much to Enterprise Performance Management (EPM), it's not easy to make it be just about a few things.

The genesis of this book is my career: For over 30 years I have been involved in Finance Systems and Processes, from my first job at Deloitte, Haskins + Sells as a 19-year-old programmer writing the Journal Entry subsystem for a trial balance program (called ATOM: Audit Techniques On Microcomputers, originally written in dBase II), through Lotus 1-2-3, Accpac, then custom-developed systems (like BOX, the Broker of Obligations and Transactions that connected US Navy purchase cards with Citibank), to nine years at Hyperion Solutions (later acquired by Oracle) where I helped raise the EPM toddler (back then it was called BPM—Business Performance Management.)

However, as they say, I am standing on the shoulders of giants with the content of this book. My EPM epiphany came after watching so many Hyperion professionals whiteboard the RAMP cycle (Report, Analyze, Model, Plan)—which I initially thought was a great way to sell software—when I started noticing clients' visceral reaction to it: "Yes! That's how I want our business to be managed!" So I immersed myself in the EPM system and started noticing all of the untapped business value. Later, I got to take that whiteboard to a whole new level with senior business executives, mostly CEOs and CFOs of name-brand companies, when I worked with Simon Tucker at The Business Foundation. When we took out the technical jargon and talked only in management processes, business value and strategy-to-execution terms, they would experience a reaction similar to my Hyperion clients: "I don't care what you call it or what it costs, *that's* what I want!"

I'd like to think of this book as part sequel to Howard Dresner's first book *The Performance Management Revolution: Business Results Through Insight and Action* (John Wiley & Sons, 2007). I had a lot of fun working on that book with Howard and this book delves into some of his ideas in more detail and with less eloquence.

Who should read this book?

This book is for CFOs, CIOs, their direct reports, and any organizational visionary or aspiring leader who wants to "bring it all together" and create an actionable vision and plan for improving performance. The book is also intended for managers who want to understand EPM and how it can help them be better managers. My hope is that any student of EPM can learn and apply at least a few ideas from this book.

If you think of your business as a giant computer, and all of your resources including time, money, people, assets, products, and customers as the data files and software applications on that computer, then what is the operating system of your business? What is it that directs, guides, prioritizes, organizes, and optimizes your resources? I call this, simply, your management operating system.

Enterprise Performance Management Done Right is essentially about three things to help you improve your management operating system:

1. **A Framework.** This is the management operating system for your business and shows how all of the pieces of EPM work together as one holistic process. It is most useful as a long-term, high-level EPM vision.
2. **Enabling Technologies.** Within the framework, I show what pieces you need to put into place to deliver on the necessary EPM processes.
3. **A Fresh EPM Roadmap.** This is insight on how to prioritize all those potential EPM initiatives given your strategic business objectives, and how they are supported by enabling technologies, eventually being fulfilled on your aspirational EPM framework.

Overview of the Content

The book is organized into nine chapters.

> **Chapter 1: What's Broken and What's Possible.** This chapter gives you an overview of the promise of EPM. It helps you understand what problems this domain was created to solve and how well it's been solving them.
>
> **Chapter 2: An Enterprise Performance Management Process.** This is the central idea of the book and of the model for "real" EPM. It's a straightforward management process that is enabled by EPM processes and technology. It's a closed-loop "uber" process that helps guide your EPM roadmap and helps deliver on the promises of EPM.
>
> **Chapter 3: Gather: Turning Data into Information.** One of the most common elements of EPM is management reporting. It helps answer the question "where are we and how are we doing" at a particular point in

time. This chapter outlines how reporting has changed to be much more dynamic, how it has to deliver more insight than ever, and how it cannot live in isolation.

Chapter 4: Understand: Turning Insights into Actions. EPM decouples analytics from reporting to become its own discipline, not just in the hands of the few. This chapter addresses the "why." Why did we get what we got? It explores approaches to understanding through business questions and includes the ideas behind "Big Data" and predictive analytics.

Chapter 5: Debate: Turning "What If" into "What's Next." One of the most overlooked cornerstones of EPM, modeling "what if" scenarios, is the topic of this chapter. Enabling a robust, fact-based, open debate in the company helps it prepare for a variety of possible futures and helps it maximize the value of its assets and minimize risk.

Chapter 6: Commit: Bringing Accountability and Focus to the Enterprise. Enterprise planning is a topic many people confuse for EPM itself. While certainly a critical part of EPM, there's more to EPM than planning. This chapter describes some better practices and shows how planning should be connected to the other areas of the management operating system.

Chapter 7: Execute: From Insight to Action to Results. Chapter 7 is a collection of EPM use cases across a variety of business functions, including Sales and Marketing, Supply Chain, and Human Resources, and processes like order-to-cash. From this chapter you'll see how EPM can be applied to any area of the business . . . not just Finance.

Chapter 8: Strategy: Aligned to the Right Outcomes. EPM works when it's aligned with, and in support of an organization's strategic objectives. Chapter 8 covers several topics on aligning EPM to strategy including the ever-popular Profitability Management.

Chapter 9: Bringing It All Together. Chapter 9 is all about developing your next-generation EPM roadmap based on the concepts and practices discussed in this book. It helps you sell EPM internally, ties up a few loose ends, and addresses what it takes to become world class in EPM adoption.

Appendix: An EPM Maturity Model. As you progress in your journey to EPM sophistication, it's useful to be able to grade yourself on where you are and where you want to be. This EPM Maturity Model can be used to facilitate discussions on agreeing on your roadmap and prioritizing EPM initiatives.

So What?

Typically, EPM is thought of as solely a Finance or Information Technology initiative and can easily be put in the "operational efficiency through automation" bucket of benefits. Which is just a fancy way of saying a corporate cost-cutting program. However, in order for EPM to really matter in the business, it has to have a direct impact on more than just operating margins. Ideally, it should provide your department, business unit, and company with one or more competitive advantages in the areas of:

- Customer acquisition and retention
- Product innovation and profitability
- People productivity
- Supply-chain efficiency
- Marketing effectiveness
- Overall sustainable execution of strategy

It is no longer an IT-led area but rather a joint IT, Finance, and Business concern that impacts all of these performance areas.

Revenue Growth

One of the first areas of the business to look at for financial performance and competitive advantage is revenue growth. There are a variety of ways EPM can improve revenue growth, including:

- Better focus on sales productivity through more relevant, expedient sales forecasting
- Better sales velocity by focusing efforts on the best-selling products, bundles, and channels
- Maximized revenue by modeling product, bundle, and channel price mixes

Operating Margin

Especially in a down economy, with the automatic reaction to cut costs, EPM can help ensure you cut the "right" costs and that the removal of those costs doesn't adversely impact profitable revenue or future market share. EPM can impact this area in many ways, for example:

- Understanding customer and product profitability allows companies to focus on marketing and selling the products that give the best return

- Quickly modeling NewCo scenarios in a pending acquisition and basing those models on historical data and actual constraints (by product, by geo, by customer segment, etc.) can give a more accurate picture of available synergies to set the expectations of the street

Cash Cycle

Accelerating your cash cycle gives you more confidence in working capital, better opportunities for investments, and improves overall efficiencies. EPM efforts can include:

- Gathering and sharing information on Days Sales Outstanding (DSO), Days Payable Outstanding (DPO), and Days in Inventory (DII)—delivered to the right people in the organization (and tied to employee rewards)—can have a positive impact on cash cycle
- Cash-Flow forecasting and Working Capital analysis can help improve the cost of capital, debt ratios, and can reduce risk

Asset Utilization

Ensuring that assets such as plants, production lines, or equipment, are being employed in profitable activities is the way of an efficient organization. A couple of ways that EPM can impact your return on assets include:

- Modeling capacity to ensure you have the right equipment availability, manpower, and output or yield
- Scheduled versus unscheduled repair analysis to show how effective your preventative maintenance programs are

Customer Satisfaction

Making sure customers are attracted to your company and products and then retained for maximum lifetime value is one of the goals of most organizations. EPM can help ensure that this happens by:

- Showing if there's a correlation between customer satisfaction levels and customer support staffing
- Analyzing customer satisfaction scores by product and product lifecycle over time, showing root causes for declines in product satisfaction
- Tracking a plan to improve Net Promoter Score by department

Employee Engagement

With more awareness and accountability, employees at all levels of the organization can make decisions to improve both the top and bottom lines.

- EPM helps show how what you're working on is related to overall targets. For example, an A/R clerk can see how the velocity of receivables under his or her control can impact DSO, working capital, and free cash flow
- EPM encourages more sharing and collaboration of plans, analyses and results, and reduces the need to recreate the wheel every time

Organic Growth and Outperformance Management

Unfortunately, many people equate EPM with enterprise budgeting/planning applications coupled with a statutory and management reporting initiative—with a focus on compliance and control. The real goal of EPM is to have a material impact on business performance, to standardize on one management operating system across an organization—for better performance visibility, execution, accountability, and organizational flexibility. What if you had a stretch goal of using EPM not just for performance management, but for OUT-performance management?

How would we use EPM to outperform your competitors on both revenue growth and profitability over the long term?

There are many ways to do this:

1. Organic growth is key—an intelligent investment in organic growth may provide more value than growth through acquisition. EPM supports organic growth in many ways:
   a. Profitability management with customer and market segmentation: spending more effort marketing and selling the most profitable product/service offerings to the right people at the right time at the right price (price modeling and analytics is a key component of this).
   b. Model, plan for, measure, and manage cross-selling and up-selling efforts. Use analytics to understand which cross-selling and up-selling initiatives work and how they can be replicated. Tie this into the pricing models as well.
   c. Look to adjacencies, for example, bundles with partner products/services (e.g., Nike + iPod). These can capture new markets and pull along sales of your products. Including external parties

(suppliers, partners, resellers) in your rolling revenue forecasting process gives you more visibility into opportunities;

    d. Market expansion: EPM includes multidimensional modeling of different scenarios that can be risk weighted, so, for example, if you want to expand to an emerging market, you can factor in risk from currency fluctuations, government regulations, and other assumptions. Once you have debated and selected the right model, you can use that as the basis for a capital expenditure plan, revenue and expense budget, and workforce plan.

2. Other areas for EPM to contribute to out-performance include supporting and interconnecting knowledge-intensive intangibles (intellectual property [IP], patents, copyrights, strong brands) to financial and operational key performance indicators (KPIs)—thus linking innovation to the entire business.

If you want a quick way to start using EPM to impact the top and bottom line, simply add a new category to your revenue forecast: from "worst-case," "probable," and "commit" to a "stretch" (upside) number, and start managing to that.

EPM, as it is currently practiced, is still largely a collection of silos. It's time to bring it all together, to interconnect the processes, to build on a common-rules and meta-data platform and to turn EPM into a sophisticated management operating system.

My hope is that you embrace the Management Operating System and use EPM to drive value for your people, your customers and vendors, your markets, and all of your stakeholders.

My hidden agenda is to help move the EPM industry forward through more sophisticated adoption and by showing more correlation to improving performance. At a minimum, that would include:

- Making it a closed-loop process, not fragmented silos and initiatives
- Encompassing all areas of the business including Sales and Marketing, Operations, and Development, not exclusive to Finance
- Including Business Intelligence and Business Analytics, not just Enterprise Planning and Reporting
- Using it as a platform for continuous improvement, better transparency, collaboration, and what author Daniel Pink says truly motivates us: Autonomy, Mastery, and Purpose[1]

Note

1. Daniel H. Pink, *Drive: The Surprising Truth About What Motivates Us* (Riverhead Press, 2009).

ACKNOWLEDGMENTS

To my friend Simon Tucker from whom I have learned much and shared many adventures and laughs. Much of the content for this book was formed and validated while working with Simon on myriad clients.

Thanks to Gebhard Rainer for his foreword—I first heard Gebhard speak at a Hyperion event in 2004 and I realized just how much difference EPM can make in a business.

To those who encouraged and supported me in writing this book: Rick Cadman, Dawna MacLean, Nancy Belmont, Tony Mayo, and my advisory board and brain trust in Tony's Vitality, Service and Outstanding Performance (VSOP) executive coaching group. A special thanks to Tony for recommending Scrivener software, which doubled my productivity overnight.

To Howard Dresner and Frank Buytendijk, who made strategy fun.

To my early mentors from Deloitte in Toronto: John Gambles, P. Howard Lyons, Jim Youldon, and Denman Lawrenson.

To Alan Slaight for letting me work on his book on Stewart James (*Stewart James in Print: The First Fifty Years* [Jogestja, 1989]).

To friends and colleagues who reviewed the content, gave me feedback, and helped improve the overall quality of the book, especially Rich Fluck, Nina Acosta, Kim Flaherty, Toby Hatch, John O'Rourke, and again, Rick Cadman.

To Oracle Corporation and Tableau Software Inc. for their screenshots.

To my editors at John Wiley & Sons: Tim Burgard and Stacey Rivera, with much gratitude for their vision and their patience.

To countless colleagues at Deloitte, ITG, Hyperion, Infosys, and Check-Point Consulting, and all those clients through 30 years of consulting that taught me their businesses and allowed me to contribute to their success.

And I want to acknowledge my family for their love, motivation, and joy. Especially my sister, Marlene, for reminding me who I am.

Ron Dimon
Fairfax, VA
April 2013

CHAPTER 1

What's Broken and What's Possible

"Finding what's wrong and fixing it" versus "seeing what's possible and going for it" give two very different lives.

—Tony Mayo

We are in the middle of an information deluge and an insight glut.[1]

Our systems, processes, and information are still struggling to escape silos when the economy is crying out for collaboration, efficiency, and better results.

Folks are constantly reinventing the wheel at work and some lament "if only people in our company knew what everyone in our company knows!"[2] Many companies can barely agree on the definition of a customer, an employee, or sales figures, let alone agree on how to improve them.

With all this technology and information at our fingertips, we are still making decisions in the dark and relying on our best guesses.

Certainly some organizations are doing better than others when it comes to closed-loop, fact-based decision-making, but the opportunity to take advantage of all this data we have is barely being exploited.

Strategy-Execution Gap

What is it that thwarts a rigorous process of sustainably executing an organization's strategy? As shown in Figure 1.1, some of the barriers include those capabilities that are the responsibility of managers and leaders in the organization.

In March 2010, *Harvard Business Review* (HBR) surveyed 1,075 HBR readers about strategy and execution in their organizations.[3] Only 37% said their companies are "very good" or "excellent" at execution.

1

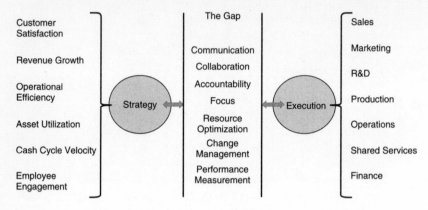

Figure 1.1   Barriers in the Strategy-Execution Gap

The HBR survey found that the top barriers to strategy-execution were:

- Making the strategy meaningful to front-liners
- Poor communication of strategy
- Lack of accountability
- Lack of clear and decisive leadership
- Too much focus on short-term results
- Everyone is too busy/not enough resources
- Resistance to change
- Strategy goals remain vague and pointless:
  - Leadership actions are inconsistent with strategy
  - Inability to measure impact
  - Business units with competing agendas
  - Too much uncertainty

In my consulting work, and being an employee for small, medium, and large organizations, I've seen some of the barriers to effective strategy execution including the following:

- No vetting of the strategy to see if it's actually doable (do we have the right capital, right products, right markets, right people?), and little debate to refine the strategy.
- Low agreement on what the strategy actually is—even among the C-suite executives (it's always a surprise to see this).
- Low connection between the corporate financial and operational business models (made in the vetting debate) and budgets, plans, and forecasts.

- Low buy-in to the budgets, plans, and forecasts (usually due to management overrides after a bottoms-up exercise), resulting in low buy-in to the strategy from lower levels in the organization.
- Low agreement on what the right measures are to see how well we're doing, and no visible connection between those measures and strategic objectives.
- Low belief that the numbers seen are accurate (or at least the same version), as well as a lot of manual effort to get at the numbers.
- Low understanding of the root causes as to why the company achieves, underachieves, or overachieves results.
- Little connection between root-cause analysis and tweaking the strategy ("hey, we are losing money on product X, and it's not a loss-leader, should we be in that business?").
- Low accountability for results. Some organizations don't have targets or owners for their key objectives.

When it does work, I've seen things like accounts receivable associates having a Business Intelligence (BI) dashboard that shows how they have a daily impact on days sales outstanding and cash collections which directly impacts strategic objectives like profitable revenue growth.

According to Roger Martin, Dean of the Rotman School of Management at the University of Toronto, in his article "The Execution Trap,"[4] as operational and front-line employees have to make decisions every day involving customers and operations, they become de facto strategists. Or, in my view, at least de facto strategy executioners, and I don't mean they have to kill the strategy!

Imagine if your number-one strategic objective is "profitable revenue growth," and the target is 10% year-over-year improvement in both revenue and operating margin. Also imagine that every employee knows this—they even have it written on a laminated card they carry around in their wallets and purses. And then one of your customer service reps gets a phone call from an irate customer. Typically, the customer service rep is measured on customer satisfaction including low call time, low time-to-resolution, high-marks on the net promoter score scale for each interaction, and so on. But what if the phone call from the irate customer was accompanied by a dashboard that automatically popped up on the customer service rep's screen that showed:

- Customer lifetime value (CLV) (how much the customers company had spent on your products and services) was 50% lower than the average CLV.
- Cost to serve (the amount spent on support, maintenance, returns, and so on) was 50% higher than the average cost to serve.

- Overall customer profitability was ranked in the bottom 10% (this customer was very good at negotiating deep discounts on prices during the end-of-quarter sales cycle).

What would your customer service rep do? Would you want them to treat the irate customer as any other customer and invest the time and money to solve their problem or concern? Or would you want the customer service rep to forward the customer call on to a special help desk that, in line with your number one strategic objective, would "fire" this customer?

We need a better management process because business-as-usual is over. In its place we have a faster-paced, rapidly changing world, including:

- A need to be more agile, more responsive, and more tolerant of uncertainty
- Better-informed customers
- Changing market and business models
- Structural changes in the economics of business
- Regulatory revolution
- Growth through acquisition as the normal course of business
- Redefining asset values
- Changing delivery channels
- Vast new information sources
- Compressed cycle times

And those compressed cycle times impact the entire business:

- Time to market for new products and services (concept to realization)
- Time to deliver to the customer
- Time to close the books
- Time to hire new staff
- Time to deploy new staff (on-boarding)
- Time for new staff to reach full productivity
- Time to make key decisions
- Time to complete major business transactions
- Time to obsolescence for equipment and products
- Time to integrate acquisitions
- Time to respond to competitive actions
- Time to return on investment (ROI) (especially for new technology investments)
- Time to enter a new market[5]

EPM was designed to fill this strategy to execution gap. It's the new approach to management that makes strategy everyone's job, that gives them the tools and processes to execute based on focus, alignment, and accountability.

Buckets of Pain

In working with my clients across a wide spectrum of business sizes, industries, and geographies, when it comes to EPM, there are some "buckets" of pain I have found common to them all:

- More time is spent on assembling the numbers than on analyzing them—all this manual effort makes us inefficient and not very scalable.
- People show up to meetings with "their" numbers, and we don't know how they got those numbers—there is not a lot of confidence.
- Some people aren't getting the reports or analyses we're sending out—it either gets lost in their email or the right people aren't on the distribution list (or they're ignoring it).
- There is little alignment across functions (Sales, Marketing, Development, HR).
- People aren't following the prescribed processes, especially for submitting their plans and forecasts—they make different assumptions and interpret what we want differently.
- The right people don't have access to the right information, at the right time.
- Sometimes the data is just plain wrong—it doesn't include the latest numbers or it's an old version, or it's missing parts.
- There is a frustrating amount of "reinventing the wheel" and lack of coordination across teams—a group will create a process or system without knowing that there's already one in place.
- The reports are static and users can't interact with them—there's no depth (drill-down) or slice-and-dice.
- Sometimes their reports, plans, analyses, and models are just too complex to understand or believe—rules and transformations have been added on over the years unchecked and unauditable.
- Some of their key measures don't even have targets, so how will they know how they're doing? And where they do know, they're not sure who's responsible for the variance.

- People are working off of different definitions (of customer, of employee, of revenue) and different formulas making it difficult to compare apples to apples.
- They have data timing problems (e.g., daily sales, monthly expenses).
- They are living in "spreadsheet hell."

These buckets of pain can be further summarized as a lack of foundational business elements as shown in Table 1.1.

Addressing this pain and implementing these foundations can be difficult. Some of the top barriers to EPM adoption include:

- Getting at, and believing in, the data. Too many managers still "torture" the data until it fits their needs, so that its credibility is lost.
- Getting managers to take action based on the data.
- The political will at the top to embrace and adopt EPM: Sometimes successful EPM implementations make careers, sometimes they break them.
- Knowing only the cost, and not the value of the effort and capital it will take to be an EPM-centric organization.
- Being complacent with some of the silo or point-solutions, like having a good planning tool and stopping there.
- Conflicting priorities and limited resources mean many managers are focused on short-term fire drills and don't spend the time to fix the root cause.

Table 1.1   A Summary of the Buckets of Pain

A lack of . . .	
Believability	I don't trust the numbers, also known as "one version of the truth" or data quality issues.
Visibility	I can't get to the numbers I need, when I need them, at the right level of detail, or they aren't fresh enough.
Focus	I have too much data and not enough actionable information.
Alignment	We are not on the same page regarding the drivers of the business.
Efficiency	Too much time spent manually extracting numbers, or on manual tie-out, or on reinventing reports and analysis that already exist.
Definitions	We don't agree on what numbers mean (e.g., Revenue—is that booked? recognized? commissionable?)
Accountability	No one is "on the hook" for the number, or the targets don't exist or are meaningless. There is no closed-loop from decision to result: Was it a good decision; did we achieve the return we imagined?

The Promise of EPM

Back in 2001, Gartner Inc. coined the term Corporate Performance Management (CPM) which promised to address these concerns with a unified management system.

What's happened since 2001?

Somehow, EPM lost its way. And it's been subverted to mean many things. Some take it to mean:

- BI
- Enterprise planning
- Connecting reporting and planning
- Balanced Scorecards

The promise was to close the loop from plan to result, from insight to action the reality is that CPM became business performance management (BPM) now EPM and really consists of three silos:

1. Enterprise planning (budgeting, planning, and forecasting),
2. Statutory consolidation, close and reporting, and
3. Business Analytics.

Yet it's much more than that.

What Enterprise/Corporate/Business Performance Management Is Not

We still see confusion at client sites, in the press, on the Web, and from vendors and consultants as to just what is EPM, CPM, BPM, or integrated performance management (IPM). No wonder there's confusion, we still can't even agree on what to call it! There are too many solutions that don't tie back to the vision and definition of EPM. Yet there are a number of good working definitions; let's look at two of them.

Lee Geishecker's original definition in 2001 (when she was with Gartner) was that CPM "is an umbrella term describing the methodologies, metrics, processes and systems used to monitor and manage an enterprise's business performance."[6]

"Monitor" is clearly in the domain of BI. It's the "manage" which has been open to interpretation. So let's look at an updated definition from David Axson:

[BPM] encompasses all the processes, information, and systems used by managers to set strategy, develop plans, monitor execution, forecast performance, and report results with a view to achieving sustainable success no matter how success may be defined.[7]

More encompassing, but still not embracing the key point. The real purpose of EPM is to *interconnect* each of those areas (and a few more) that Axson points out in order to align strategy with *sustainable* execution. So EPM answers the questions: "What should we do, and how should we do it," and "How did we do and why did it happen?" And it interrelates those answers.

Let's have a quick look at what EPM is not:

- It's not Balanced Scorecards. Bob Paladino's book *Five Key Principles of Corporate Performance Management* is essentially a scorecard book. There is valuable information in that book about scorecards, and while scorecards are certainly an ingredient of EPM, there is more to EPM than scorecards.
- It's not Enterprise Budgeting, Planning and Forecasting as most EPM case studies will have you believe. Although Enterprise Planning is considered the cornerstone of EPM, it alone is not EPM.
- It is not BI 2.0, and the primary components of BI are encompassed in EPM.
- It's not BPM or Enterprise Project Management. These are just unfortunate collisions of acronyms.
- It's not KPIs. But, of course, there are KPIs in EPM.
- It's not management reporting. Just another ingredient. Same for financial consolidation and statutory reporting.
- It is not the HR process of performance reviews and compensation generally referred to as performance management, they just got the *PM* acronym first.

I'll talk more about the key interconnections that truly deliver on the promise of EPM in Chapter 2.

This book shows a way to get back on track to the original vision of EPM and to use it for competitive advantage and better business results.

I was delighted to be involved in the early conversations about forming BPM at Hyperion Solutions, and was fortunate enough to be included in writing and editing one of the first books on the subject, *On the Up and Up*.[8] Table 1.2 revisits the nine tenets of a performance-accountable organization from that book to see where things stand.[9]

Table 1.2 Nine Tenets of a Performance-Accountable Organization

The Aspiration in 2004	Where We Are Today
Finds truth in numbers—A single version of the truth guides performance at all levels of the organization.	There is still a constant struggle in organizations to determine "whose numbers are right?" This problem gets worse as it gets easier to spin-off your own "spread mart" or database. Perhaps, as Frank Buytendijk says, we need to focus on one context of the truth.[10]
Sets accurate expectations—Every part of the business is directed by a shared commitment to strategic goals.	Much work has been done to communicate targets internally, yet the trend for publicly traded companies is to shy away from external guidance.
Anticipates results—A thorough understanding of business drivers and performance indicators leads to an ability to anticipate results.	More businesses are adapting driver-based planning and are focusing on the top dozen KPIs, not hundreds of metrics.
Plans with impact—Insight and dynamic processes produce actionable plans that continually guide the organization to success in changing conditions.	Rolling forecasts and more frequent planning cycles are in place at many companies. Operational and Financial planning are coming together.
Achieves on-demand visibility—A system that combines data from existing transactional systems across the enterprise gives managers transparent access to performance information anytime, anywhere.	BI has taken off, yet there is much more to be done for user adoption. Mobile BI is helping that.
Delivers continuous improvement—A commitment to knowledge and understanding produces insight that drives continuous performance improvement.	This is the ripest area for exploitation in EPM. Feedback from the planning cycle sometimes makes its way into models and scenarios, but, as one client says, "corporate has no memory."
Reports with confidence—Detailed, integrated and accessible financial and operational information enables executives to personally certify business results.	Sarbanes-Oxley attestation requirements have done much to propel external reporting standards. Yet fraud, waste, and abuse abound!
Executes with conviction—Truth, clarity, and confidence forge a powerful link between strategy, plans, and execution.	Fact-based decision-making is on the rise.[11]
Stands up to scrutiny—A comprehensive approach to Business Performance Management meets the highest standards of accountability and confidence.	There is even more demand for transparency.

Think of ERP as "run the business," and EPM as "manage the business" as shown in Figure 1.2.

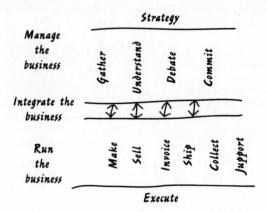

Figure 1.2   Manage the Business versus Run the Business

You run the business with all of the day-to-day transactions and processes your company performs including:

- Order to cash
- Procure to pay
- Request to resolution/service to satisfaction
- Plan to stock
- Concept to product
- Acquire to retire (fixed assets)
- Hire to retire (human resources)

You have probably invested a lot of time, energy, and money in "run the business" with myriad transactional systems, including:

- ERP including general ledgers, accounts receivable, accounts payable, fixed assets and so on
- Customer relationship management (CRM)
- Supply chain management (SCM)
- Sales force automation (SFA)
- Human resource information systems (HRIS)
- Product lifecycle management (PLM)

And usually many more legacy or custom transactions systems to track everything from contracts to commissions.

And on top of them all—I say "on top" to mean at a level of abstraction above the details—are the decisions, processes, and information needed to manage the business (see Table 1.3).

Table 1.3 Differences between "Run the Business" and "Manage the Business"

Run the Business	Manage the Business
Transactional	Consolidated
Detailed	Summarized
Real time	Periodic (weekly/monthly)
Tactical	Strategic
Front lines/back office	Managers/executives

Having the distinction between run the business and manage the business allows your organization, especially IT, to focus on the different processes, technologies, and information that need to belong in both domains.

But why bother? What difference does EPM make in your business? You can look at the benefits of EPM in different ways:

1. **Management Efficiency.** EPM enables standard management processes that every company must do well:
   - Budgeting, planning and forecasting
   - Financial consolidation and statutory reporting
   - Management reporting and business intelligence
   - Profitability analysis, and
   - Other financial and operational modeling, planning, analysis, and reporting

   EPM leverages the investment you have already made in Enterprise Resource Management, Customer Relationship Management, Supply Chain Management, Sales Force Automation, and other transactional systems.

2. **Executing Strategy.** EPM can help close the loop between what you want to happen in the business (and how), and what actually happened (and why):
   - Records and documents business model assumptions, constraints, and drivers
   - Connects those models into your annual operating plans, budgets, and forecasts
   - Monitors and alerts exceptional variances from actual to plan
   - Helps you understand the root causes of variance and plug that corporate knowledge back into the business model and strategy
   - Ties it all together with a common business language and common master data to improve visibility, focus, and alignment
   - Giving more stakeholder alignment

3. **Improving Performance.** EPM can have a material impact on the top and bottom line, on the balance sheet, and on overall return on capital:
   - It can improve visibility into the key drivers of value in the business.
   - It can show the cause and effect relationship of operational metrics on financial performance.
   - It helps you focus on the right things in the business.
   - It can bring agility to business models and organizational structures.

   Giving better business decisions that are based on more timely information

4. **Reducing Risk.** By improving transparency and the right access to information, managers can see for themselves where the business is and can test operational and financial models to help make the best resource deployment decisions:
   - Global governance and compliance of data and reporting
   - It adds a level of accountability for results
   - Better preparation for change, increased predictability
   - Fewer surprises through better collaboration and communication

5. **Competitive Advantage.** Organizations that get EPM right are more nimble than those who don't.
   - Better strategy formulation and planning
   - Less complexity and lower costs by unifying management information
   - Increased organizational flexibility (mergers and acquisitions, organizational changes)

"Business Intelligence with a Purpose"

This was the phrase that Howard Dresner used to help describe EPM in the early days.

Since BI is more prevalent in the vernacular of CIOs and business managers, it's a good term to use to help enroll people in the idea of decision support, analytics, and reporting.

Some people that think EPM is really BI "plus" (the plus is usually Planning), and some think BI is independent of EPM. Vendor product strategies also ended up driving the definition of EPM: Those that have a BI offering include it in the definition, those that don't, well, don't. Yet I don't think it matters what it's called. What matters is the value it delivers, whatever it's called. As a business manager or technologist, if calling EPM "BI" helps enroll others in your organization about the possibility of using information for better fact-based decisions, resource utilization and accountability, then by all means use that term. However, I would suggest that once you have enrolled them in the term, make sure they understand your point of view, which, if this book does its job, will include a closed-loop management process and the components of EPM in that vision.

If I were on an elevator[12] with an executive of the company I worked at, and was asked what I was working on, here's what I would say:

> I'm working on building a common business process we can all use to execute our strategy. So we can agree on the results we're getting, who's on the hook, and tying that together with our plans so we can all focus on the right things, rowing in the same direction.

What would you say?

Notes

1. "Data, Data Everywhere," *The Economist*, February 25, 2010, www.economist.com/node/15557443, retrieved October 16, 2012.
2. I first heard this expression from Godfrey Sullivan, then CEO of Hyperion Solutions. It's meant to express the frustration of information silos and the longing to unlock the value of shared intelligence. For example, when pursuing a new prospect, wouldn't it be good to know how employees in your company may be connected to employees in the prospect company?
3. "How Hierarchy Can Hurt Strategy Execution," *Harvard Business Review*, July 2010, http://hbr.org/2010/07/how-hierarchy-can-hurt-strategy-execution/ar/1, retrieved October 16, 2012.
4. Roger L. Martin, "The Execution Trap," *Harvard Business Review*, July–August 2010, http://hbr.org/2010/07/the-execution-trap/ar/1, retrieved November 16, 2012.
5. David Axson, *Best Practices in Planning and Performance Management*, John Wiley & Sons, 2007.
6. Lee Geishecker and Nigel Rayner, *Corporate Performance Management: BI Collides With ERP*, Research Note SPA-14-9282, Gartner, Inc., December 17, 2001.
7. David Axson, *Best Practices in Planning and Performance Management*, John Wiley & Sons, 2007, p. 24.
8. Kathi Fox, Jeff Rodek, et al., *On the Up and Up*, Hyperion, 2004.
9. Ibid. p. 111.
10. Frank Buytendijk, *Performance Leadership*, McGraw-Hill, 2008, Chapter 6.
11. Tom Davenport and Jeanne Harris, *Competing on Analytics: The New Science of Winning*, Harvard Business School, 2007.
12. I was once on the elevator with my client, the director of Financial Planning and Analysis, who was in charge of EPM projects at a major health care company in Los Angeles. Lo and behold, the CEO walks in to the elevator, notices her—and me with her—and he asks her what she's working on. Here's her chance to elevate the EPM conversation to the strategic import it deserves, to get the attention of the perfect EPM champion, and to ensure her future EPM projects are supported and well-funded. To my shock and dismay, her reply was: "Nothing."

CHAPTER 2

An Enterprise Performance Management Process

It is not the strongest of the species that survives, nor the most intelligent, but the one most responsive to change.

—CHARLES DARWIN

You have a lot of data. Tons of it. And you're getting more every day.[1] The trick is to turn that data into information that will help you take some action to further your goals.

Data comes from a wide variety of places these days:

- Structured transactional systems (internal and external)
  - See the list under Run the Business in Table 1.3 in Chapter 1
  - Rate services (foreign currency rates, interest rates, economic indicators)
  - Myriad "legacy" systems
  - Partner systems (e.g., a supplier's inventory system)
- Unstructured internal systems
  - Email and calendars
  - Documents, spreadsheets, PowerPoint files
  - Notes, annotations, announcements
- Unstructured external systems
  - Twitter
  - Blogs and comments
  - Facebook
  - Newswires
  - Websites

So how do you make sense and meaning of it all? How do you make it useful and work for you?

Context

First we need some context. A number doesn't actually mean anything by itself. 127 could mean anything. It's not until you know more attributes about the number that you can do anything about it.

Some of the most common attributes of numbers in EPM include:

- **Units.** This could be dollars, volumes, days, and so on. Let's say 127 means dollars for this exercise.
- **Account.** For example, sales, travel expenses, headcount. So $127 could be your travel expenses.
- **Currency.** Especially for multinational companies, you need to know which currency we're talking about. Let's say in this example, it's $CDN127.
- **Time period.** It could be for a year, a month, a week, a day. $CDN127 in travel expenses for February.
- **Organization unit.** That $CDN127 could belong to our marketing organization or to a specific cost center or even right down to a person.
- **Geography.** While this can sometimes be part of the organizational org. unit, it can also stand alone—especially when organizational units are duplicated across geographies. Perhaps our $CDN127 is a travel expense belonging to our Dutch marketing department—on a trip from Amsterdam to Toronto, one of our product specialists took a client to dinner.
- **Product.** Perhaps our product specialist focuses on a specific product and all of her travel expenses relate directly to that product (as opposed to general overhead).
- **Scenario.** Is this number the actual number, that is, the amount actually incurred, or the budgeted number? Is it proforma U.S. generally accepted accounting standards (GAAP), or International Financial Reporting Standards (IFRS)?
- **Other attributes.** These include customer, channel, employee, and so on.

So in our example, 127 can be the actual Canadian dollars our Dutch marketing department spent to help sell product X to customer A. Now I have a context for the number, but I still don't know what it means—is it good, or bad?

Good or bad depends on at least two things: what your expectations were and what results were produced. If your budget for customer meals for the trip was $CDN500, then 127 is good—it's under budget. However, if your budget of $500 was expected to generate follow-on sales of $10,000 and that did not happen with the customer you took out to dinner, you didn't meet your objectives and that's bad.

This context is very important in all aspects of EPM. It gives us our point of view on the information we are consuming and contributing yet allows us to be part of the enterprise-wide collection of information and insights. We'll explore this multidimensionality of EPM later in Chapter 4.

Impact

So for all of that data we have, how do we weed through it and focus only on the bad results that we have to do something about and the good results we want to acknowledge and duplicate?

In order to do that, we have to ascribe value to the attributes of our data. What makes your data important? Here are a few things to look at:

- **Materiality.** Does the data have a material impact on your business? Examples include sales, gross margin, product quality, customer satisfaction, labor expense, and so on.
- **Volatility.** Does the data change frequently and can it fluctuate wildly? Some commodity prices are highly volatile, while most employee satisfaction survey results aren't. Volatility can add urgency to importance.
- **Variance.** How does the data compare to what you planned the result to be, and what is your tolerance for that variation? You may have a plus or minus 5% tolerance on overhead expenses, and a 15% tolerance on sales forecast (since sales forecasts are notoriously difficult to reign in, right?)
- **Reach.** Does the data need to be seen by many people in the organization? Data that is seen by more people needs to be more frequent, of high quality, and tends to impact many business decisions.
- **Affect.** Does that data affect other data in the business? Our travel expense affects our selling, general, and administrative (SG&A) expense and our operating margin. It may also affect end-of-month discretionary spend and even variable compensation (we don't get our bonus if we exceed expense budgets for example).

Responsibility

Even if you understand the context of the data and it has impact on the business, it may not be important to you because it's not in your area of

Table 2.1 A Business Function and Layer Matrix

	Mar-keting	Sales	Custo-mer Care	Research and Develop-ment	Human Resour-ces	Infor-mation Techno-logy	Finance
Strategic							
Operational							
Tactical							

control or responsibility. As a territory sales manager, you are focused on sales (and maybe margin), headcount, quota, and the like. You probably aren't that interested in commodity prices or days payable outstanding. A simple and effective way to think about areas of responsibility is a functional matrix[2] of the business as shown in Table 2.1.

People that work in the Marketing function at the Strategic layer, like the Chief Marketing Officer (CMO), care about different things than the accounts receivable clerk who works at the Tactical layer of Finance. The interesting thing is that the different things they care about may be more related than they think—more on that later in Chapter 8 under Functional Value Maps. This is also a useful way to look at things when we consider EPM and BI tools (in Chapter 3, Table 3.3, Matching the Tool to the Type of User), since people at different levels of the organization consume data differently.

Management Operating System

Now that we've got context, impact, and responsibility out of the way, I can introduce a framework for thinking about EPM and BI.

The genesis of this framework came from my days working at Hyperion Solutions (later acquired by Oracle Corp.) and was refined and expanded when I worked with Simon Tucker at Business Foundation Corporation.

It's been called a management "operating system" for your company because, like the operating system of your computer, it helps govern input and output and manage what applications (or decisions) are being run and helps make the most effective use of resources (memory, disk space, CPU cycles).

The closed-loop system is shown in Figure 2.1.

In order to describe it, let's get into the details. You can start anywhere on this closed-loop to tell the management operating system story, and I'll start with Gather—the most common part of the cycle.

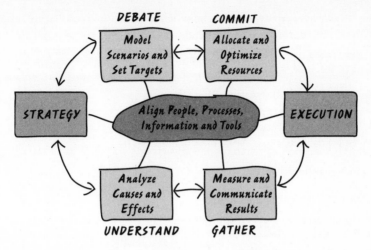

Figure 2.1   Management Operating System: High-Level

Gather

While you are busy running your business (Execute), you are generating data. You gather that data into useful information (according to its context) and deliver it to the right people (according to impact and areas of responsibility).

This is the place where managers consume reports about the results of the business, as shown in Figure 2.2. Depending on your industry and your business, there are generally two kinds of reports: mostly financial and mostly operational. The trend has been to combine financial and operational information on one report, which is a good idea since the two are

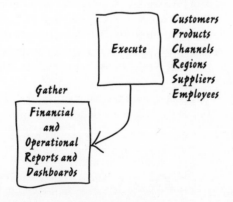

Figure 2.2   Start of the Cycle

interrelated: financial investments help drive operational results, and effective operations help contribute to financial performance.

Reports are delivered in a variety of formats with a variety of tools and can be categorized as:

- Canned (static) reports
- Ad hoc or interactive reports
- Dashboards and scorecards
- Spreadsheets

Some examples include:

Primarily financial in nature
- Quarterly business review packages
- Sales dashboards
- Line-of-business profit and loss
- Accounts receivable aging reports
- Daily cash position

Primarily operational in nature
- Employee health and safety status report
- Open headcount report
- Customer returns
- Product failure report
- Utilization report

Where Are We?

Gathering all of this data into useful financial and operational reporting helps answer the question "where are we?" Reports give their readers a snapshot of what results have been produced to date to help them gauge how close to their goals and targets they are. In order for that to happen, reports generally have to compare actual results to planned performance. Much more on this later in Chapter 4.

Also, in order for readers to gauge where they are, the information on the report has to be relevant. Relevance depends on a lot of variables, some of which include:

- The right metrics (measures that matter to you)
- Timeliness (not giving sales managers weekly sales numbers from two months ago)
- The right level of detail (appropriate to my role, and my needs to answer business questions)

- The right variance (actuals versus plan or versus forecast (or both), actuals versus prior period, and so on)
- The right dimensions (e.g., monthly and year-to-date sales by product, by region)

A great report will also help guide you on where you need to pay attention. It will alert you to places where the variance is too far out of tolerance and will have the most impact on the business.

Understand

Okay, you have gathered all the most useful data and turned it into reports that deliver the right information to the right people at the right time. Now you want to know what it means.

The next stage of the cycle is where you look more deeply into the results reported and understand the causes and potential implications of the results (see Figure 2.3).

Understand includes both financial and operational analysis. Types of analytics include:

- **Benchmarking.** Comparing results with internal benchmarks (those produced by other lines of business within your company) and external benchmarks (those produced by peers in your industry);
- **Trending and Correlation.** Showing whether your results are improving or not over time and compared to related measures that may be improving or not. For example, sales volume over the last three months could be improving, but total revenue could be declining because average selling price is declining;
- **Seasonality.** Comparing current results to prior results adjusted for the selling seasons of the business (e.g., retail in December, hospitality in summer);
- **Statistical.** Including regression analysis, ranking, correlation, and time series analysis.

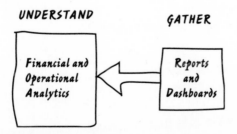

Figure 2.3   Understanding Your Results

Why Did We Get What We Got?

Analytics is about unlocking the value of the data to give us new insights into our organizations. Uncovering root causes and revealing correlations helps answer the question: "Why did we get what we got?"

One way to unlock value is to look for patterns in the data. These may include:

- Outliers (deviations from the norm, anomalies)
- Repetition (e.g., high call volumes always occur weekdays at 14:00 GMT)
- Dependency relationships (when one thing happens or changes, another thing happens or changes—in the same direction, or the opposite direction)
- Clustering relationships (uncovering independent relationships)
- Changes from the norm (sudden change in direction, changes in magnitude)

There are a variety of methods used to help uncover these patterns, including:

- **Data Visualization.** Graphical representations of the data across multiple dimensions and variables.
- **Hierarchies.** Establishing the parent/child relationships of data (this is key to successful EPM, more on this later in Chapter 4, in the discussion on multidimensional cubes).
- **Drill down.** The ability to move into further detail from the parent to child relationships to help uncover root causes of anomalies.
- **Slice and dice.** The ability to pivot the dimensions of the data on-the-fly. For example, show sales by channel and by region and zoom into the top performing region and show sales by product for that region.
- **Segmentation.** Grouping data with common attributes, especially useful for things like customer segmentation by customer type (e.g., small business, enterprise business, government, etc.)

A popular application of EPM analytics is profitability, such as in these areas:

- Company profitability
- Line-of-business profitability
- Product profitability
- Channel profitability
- Customer profitability
- Segment profitability

The benefits and challenges of profitability analytics will be discussed in more detail in Chapter 8.

Predictive analytics is another branch of the Understand stage that takes what we know has happened plus what we have seen happen in prior periods or in peer organizations, and extrapolates possible future results. Predictive analytics are especially useful for the next stage of the management cycle.

Debate

So by now we have gathered all of our data into useful information and understood our results and we have found some new insights about our businesses. Now what are we going to do about it? We want to choose the best course of action to take to either fix a problem or improve on a positive result. What's the best course of action? A robust management operating system would have us conduct a collaborative, transparent, fact-based debate about our options until we uncover and agree on the one that will give us optimal results (see Figure 2.4).

We do this all the time. Sometimes we call it what-if ("What if we drop prices by 10%?" "What if we acquire company X?"). Sometimes we call it scenario planning, and sometimes we call it business modeling. The EPM management operating system asks us to do this overtly, in a structured way, with the same level of rigor and discipline that we do reporting.

The debate consists of a variety of financial and operational models, or scenarios, each with a set of interrelated variables, or drivers, that can affect the outcome we want. The model contains business rules usually based on observable facts from historical data (e.g., when we drop the prices of certain

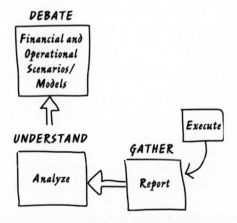

Figure 2.4   Debate Possible Scenarios

products by 10%, the sales volume for those prices increases by 7%, and the sales volume of cross-sell products increases by 12%).

Successful EPM what-if models have a few key ingredients:

- The business rules as mentioned earlier
- A blend of financial and operational drivers
- Outcomes
- Assumptions
- Constraints

In Chapter 5 we'll see how advanced EPM organizations have their models continually learn from new results and insights obtained in all stages of the management operating system.

So what are we debating and how do we pick the model?

What Do We Want to Happen?

The answer depends on what outcomes you want. Outcomes are initially driven by the strategic objectives of the organization. For most of my clients, I've noticed strategic objectives usually sound like operational targets and are expressed in the following six categories:

1. Profitable revenue growth
2. Operational efficiency (which is a euphemism for cost reduction)
3. Asset utilization
4. Improved cash flow
5. Customer satisfaction
6. Employee effectiveness/productivity

After that, the next area that drives priorities is pain. Where is the organization experiencing the most pain? Organizational pain usually equates to areas where you are furthest off target in one or more of the six categories just mentioned.

The most common pain I hear is about revenue growth—the top line (and surprisingly not profitable revenue growth). Let's take a revenue growth scenario through the first three stages of the management operating system to see how we tackle the debate.

Let's say our quarterly sales report shows that our overall sales results are 5% under where we forecasted them to be (Gather). We drill into the details and find that each sales territory is meeting its forecast except one, our largest territory (Understand).We look into sales productivity measures (sales by territory divided by quota carrying sales rep headcount by territory) and find that for our largest territory that sales productivity lags the national average by 20% (Understand). We go to the headcount report (Gather) and find a spike in unexpected attrition. Now we know the root cause: We have lost a material number of sales reps this quarter. Usually this sort of problem surfaces early in weekly sales calls, but in this example, the attrition was across multiple, uncoordinated sales teams and wasn't escalated to the territory VP appropriately. Now we know the problem, what do we want to do about it?

First, we understand that we have to get sales revenue back in line to our annual forecast and make up for the 5% shortfall this quarter. What are our options?

1. Hire more sales reps immediately to replace the lost headcount (however, there is a three-month ramp time to get a sales rep up to speed to make quota).
2. Shift some quota to other territories (and stretch the rest of the sales ranks).
3. Incent the channel to pick up the slack with new promotions.
4. Increase discounting and/or drop prices to increase sales velocity (bring some expected sales from the next quarter into this one).
5. Improve cross-sell and up-sell incentives to motivate other sales reps to overachieve their quota (pay to make up the difference in sales).
6. Reset investor expectations about the annual sales target (take your medicine).
7. Acquire a competitor to "buy" revenue attainment (make a long-term investment decision to satisfy short-term investors).

And I'm sure you can think of other options. The promise of EPM is to make the debate fact-based and to quickly understand the impact of enacting each one of these scenarios. Of course, to do that, you have to have modeled each scenario with the right drivers, rules, constraints, and assumptions. We'll get to the "how" in Chapter 5.

Assuming the "right" scenario emerges that satisfies your objectives and is doable and sustainable, the next thing the management operating system tells us to do is instantiate that choice in a plan of action and deploy our resources (human, financial, market) appropriately.

Commit

The last part of the closed-loop management operating system is called Commit. This is where the scenario you created in the Debate gets turned into a set of actionable plans that have an owner, a target, and a timeframe (see Figure 2.5).

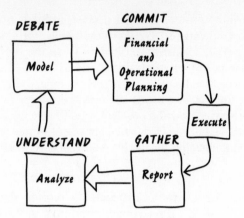

Figure 2.5   Accountable Commitments

Commitments are entrenched in an organization's financial and operation plans. The most popular kinds of plans include:

- Corporate budgets
- Annual operating plan (AOP)
- The sales plan and sales forecast
- The expense plan and expense forecast
- Workforce plan
- Compensation plan
- Commission plan
- Capital expenditure (CAPEX) plan
- Marketing plan
- Production plans
- Product lifecycle plans
- Cash-flow forecast

Many consider enterprise planning to be the heart of EPM because without a plan, how do you know how well you are performing? The details on planning will be examined in Chapter 6.

How Will We Get It Done?

Plans tell you who is accountable to deliver what, by when. A sales forecast, for example, shows each individual sales reps quota and estimated forecast (sometimes "worst case," "best case," and "commit") and sometimes by product for a given month. All reps roll up into territories, regions, and countries (or however the sales force is organized) for a "top of the house" forecast. So each sales rep knows what he or she is on the hook for in any given month.

A plan helps us optimize our resources and document how we are deploying our resources for a given period of time. Sometimes a plan is dictated from the top (top down) and sometimes it's built from the ground up (bottom up), and sometimes it's a hybrid of the two: A target is set from the top and distributed down, what's possible from the bottom-up is consolidated and the two numbers meet in the middle. The final plan is usually a negotiated amalgam of the top-down and bottom-up.

So the next step in our management operating system is to go Execute on our plan! Some of the activities that occur in execution include:

- Convert prospects to customers
- Sell products and services to customers
- Design, manufacture, and deliver new products and services
- Invoice and collect cash
- Make investments in property, plant, equipment
- Pay vendors
- Stock inventory
- Attract and retain the right workforce
- Recruit and ready sales channels and partners
- Serve customers throughout their lifecycle

When we Gather information and report on it, we are usually showing a variance of actual results to plan or forecast. Depending on our tolerance levels, some variances are fine, and others are alerts for us to take action.

Macro and Micro

The management operating system or EPM process, as some have called it, is an ongoing, closed-loop process—it doesn't really start anywhere; you're constantly in it. The interesting thing about it is that it works at a variety of levels in the organization. For example:

- At the corporate level for managing the business and for mergers, acquisitions, and divestiture decisions, and for tracking the follow-on synergies
- At the business-unit level for managing financial and operational performance to targets and for continuous improvement efforts
- At the department level for managing revenue, expense, headcount and all the relevant drivers of profitability

- At the team level for holding accountability for results, improving resource deployment decisions, and improving managerial effectiveness
- At the individual level for monitoring where you are against goals, adjusting your forecasts, and testing assumptions for coming up with new ideas and plans

Some clients have called it their decision management system, and I think it's more than that. Some have called it their performance intelligence system, and one company has even given it its own acronym, GADDiE, which stands for Gather, Analyze, Debate, Decide, Execute.[3] This eventually became both a verb and a noun in the company vernacular: "Did you GADDiE that plan?" and "Have you run that through a GADDiE?"

If you're like most of my clients, you're already doing each of these components in various places throughout the organization, to various degrees of success:

- Reporting: You have lots of them (and an average of four to five tools running them)
- Analytics: You have some smart people doing this through brute force or using some advanced tools
- Modeling: Usually reserved for corporate development types or done in spreadsheets throughout the company
- Planning: Maybe one system for the annual plan, and another for forecasting, but most of you probably still use Excel

If there's an EPM nirvana, it would be to join all of these processes, tools, data, and people together to make a complete, closed-loop, management system out of it all. And you can start anywhere.

The Middle

So that's the value of the middle of the management operating system: to bring together all of these disparate bits, to keep you from reinventing the wheel, and to automate the processes of making management decisions that impact the performance of your organization.

As shown in Figure 2.6, by bringing together the parts of the management operating system you can start to build a common business language in your organization (where everyone agrees on the definition and current actuals of recognized revenue, for example). You can corral the "shadow" IT that has

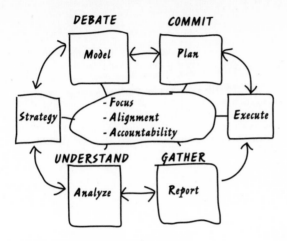

Figure 2.6   Bringing It All Together

built up to address shortcomings in centralized enterprise systems. And you can start to collaborate on end-to-end business management.

The middle will be explored more in Chapter 9.

Summary

The real value of EPM depends on a new management operating system to help unify all of the disparate pieces and point-solutions for making fact-based resource optimized decisions. If ERP was the new discipline to run the business, EPM is the new discipline to manage the business.

You are probably doing many of these pieces now. You have a lot of reporting, you analyze results when you can, someone, somewhere in Finance is running models, and you have plans. However, most of these are independent processes running on disparate technologies (mostly spreadsheets), with rampant reinventing the wheel and little collaboration or coordination.

With the management operating system framework as a way to guide the integration of these pieces into an EPM ecosystem, less time will be spent on gathering data and massaging it into useful information, or on pointing fingers, and more time will be spent on making better decisions, more effectively deploying resources, and preparing to adjust to market and economic changes.

In subsequent chapters, we'll explore each part of this new discipline in detail and give ideas and examples on the why and how to exploit EPM in your organization.

Notes

1. The Fifth Annual IDC Digital Universe Study in 2011 predicted that 1.8 zettabytes—or 1.8 trillion gigabytes—of data was created that year, and that data will grow by 50x in the next decade.
2. This matrix was first introduced to me by my friend and colleague Simon Tucker. It's a very useful way to show how information silos must be opened up if you want to improve performance—it's a holistic look at the organization.
3. This client changed Commit to Decide to emphasize that managers' decisions have to be aligned with the overall cycle and that some action has to be taken.

CHAPTER 3

Gather: Turning Data into Information

A good decision is based on knowledge and not on numbers.

—PLATO

The most common process in the management cycle from Chapter 2 is Gather. Organizations spend an incredible amount of time gathering data and trying to turn it into meaningful reports, dashboards, scorecards, and spreadsheets. In other words, turning numbers into knowledge. The purpose of all this activity is to find out where you are performing well and where you need to make some changes.

However, with the plethora of data we're getting, and with the speed at which change happens and transactions occur, it's getting harder to find out exactly where you stand. How, when, where, and why we consume data is undergoing a major shift, as shown in Table 3.1.

We have too much data and not enough information. As EPM practitioners, our job is to help deliver better insights to the business, and the starting place is useful information: on time, at the right level of detail, to the person who can use it to make a decision that helps improve short and long-term results.

If we look at the Gather process within the management operating system in more detail, as shown in Figure 3.1, we see:

- **Actuals.** Details come in from transactional systems and are correlated, "normalized," consolidated, converted, and presented in a consumable way.
- **Gaps.** Going through financial and operational reporting, if aligned with the drivers and metrics of the business, will expose gaps in transactional data that need to be addressed in other systems (like enterprise resource planning [ERP], the general ledger [G/L], customer relationship management [CRM], and so on).

Table 3.1   Data Consumption Is Undergoing a Major Shift

From	To
Static	Dynamic
A big binder or a large PDF file	When and where you need it (online, interactive, mobile)
Financial	Financial, operational, strategic
Lagging indicators	Leading indicators
Stale data	Real-time information
Fixed	Variable based on my role and my point of view
Passive	Actionable, guided
Grids of numbers	Graphical visualization
Pull (I have to go get it)	Push (it comes to me)

- **Plan data.** Rarely stored in transactional systems, budget, plan and forecast data is married with actuals data here.
- **Variance.** Variance to plan, comparisons to prior periods or internal and external benchmarks, and highlights of major (material) gaps are visible in the Gather process.
- **Financial and operational reporting interconnected.** It is becoming increasingly common to have both kinds of information blended in the same report (e.g., productivity reporting includes revenue and headcount).
- **Analysis.** The same data and metadata is used to analyze root-causes and to see trends and other patterns (see Chapter 4). Usually one

Figure 3.1   Close-Up of Gather Process and Its Inputs and Outputs

drills-down into these details directly from the Gather (reporting) process.

- **Self serve.** During an analysis, users will want more information and can come back to the Gather process to find and select relevant information to aid in understanding results and variances.

Right now, most executives get the information they ask for. What they usually don't know is the level of effort—especially manual effort—that goes into getting them the information they want. Managers and analysts in Finance and IT know only too well how much time and work it takes to assemble, verify, and deliver the needed information. I had one executive describe the solution to the problem as either automating the transformation of data into useful information, or "adding more gerbils" to spin more wheels of the manual reporting factory!

Successful gathering transforms the raw data into useful management information and lets you focus on what needs your immediate attention. With all that data, how do you know what's urgent and important versus what's interesting or worse, distracting?

Management by Exception

Most organizations have their standard "canned" reports that are reused throughout the layers of the business every week, month, and year. These are the reports that managers have identified as "meat and potatoes" for managing the business. They might include, for example:

- Monthly sales variance report
- Profit-center P&L report
- Shipment volumes by product
- Accounts receivable aging report

Instead of having to wade through a fifty-page report and figure out if you're performing well or not, mature EPM organizations alert their managers to the most material areas with the widest variances.

Managers also have their "soup-du-jour" reports that change depending on the area of focus, the burning platform, or the problem to be solved this quarter. While these can also be canned and centralized, they are more often ad hoc, where a manager can interact with the data and build the report on-the-fly to satisfy the particular need.

For more on the "meat and potatoes" and "soup-du-jour" reports, see Chapter 8.

Push and Pull

In the case of canned reports and alerts, these are "pushed" out to the manager on a periodic or real-time basis, whereas ad hoc reporting requires the manager to "pull" the information out of repositories or systems for themselves.

One of the problems I've noticed with pushed reports is that there are so many of them that aren't used anymore. Resources are stretched thin these days and many report requests are last minute, urgent, and sort of like spaghetti thrown up against the wall (to see what sticks). Over time, after the fire has been put out, or a new fire has taken its place, that report is no longer needed. Yet there may not be a process for removing reports, so it just keeps getting generated and pushed out.

Except for statutory reporting (which is discussed later in this chapter), Pull is usually a better approach. It also goes by the term "self serve." Self-serve reporting is:

- **Interactive.** Users can focus on specific areas of concern as business questions require, choosing some columns and rows over others, changing the point of view, and drilling into details where available.
- **Adaptable.** Reports change as the data changes, highlighting variances that go beyond tolerances and automatically adding detail when they do.
- **Tailored.** Reports can be specific to a user based on their security settings and their profiles. For example, if the Mid-Atlantic sales manager is using the system, only data for the Mid-Atlantic sales team appears.
- **Reusable.** Once a self-serve report is "done" (the user has the right information in the report), it can be saved for reuse later, shared with other colleagues (without having to send all the data, just the structure of the report, which will refetch the data when run by another user), and copied as a template for another report.

Ingredients

To turn raw data into useful information that you interact with, you need at least the following ingredients:

- A purpose or business question to answer (e.g., "What are our sales by region?" or "Who are our top customers?")
- A point of view for the consumer of the information (board, corporate, strategic business unit, line of business, division, team, territory, external)

- Built-in relationships—hierarchies, dimensions including time periods, apples-to-apples like currency translations, and context—year-to-date, actual vs. plan, etc.
- The right level of detail (according to business questions and consumer)
- The right metrics—whether it's a financial account like revenue, or an operational driver like headcount or a key performance indicator (KPI) or a ratio like productivity, it has to fit the business question
- Timelines—the information has to be delivered and consumed in time to do something about it
- Some comparative information—a variance to the plan or to a prior period or a benchmark
- The right way to deliver the information to the consumer (the right tool and platform)

Your Point of View

Effective information consumption takes into account several interrelated dimensions. In order to be useful, information must take into account:

- Who you are (your role in the organization)
- What you're trying to do (either answering a business question or giving you some actionable insight)
- What details you need including for which time periods you need them

To start turning data into useful information, we need to break it out by appropriate audience. One way to think of this is by categorizing groups of users into their personae. Instead of addressing each individual job category in your organization chart, you can use the framework presented in Chapter 2 as a way to classify personae. While not exhaustive, and different for every organization, the personae in Table 3.2 is representative of many organizations.

Table 3.2 shows the types of titles that "live" at the intersection of a business function (Marketing, Sales, etc.) and the layer of the business (Strategy, Operations, etc.).

So for example, in Table 3.2, the Chief Operating Officer, Chief Development Officer, and VP of Manufacturing would all share one persona: Strategic Management of Development and Delivery.

The fact that they live in the same intersection of the organization assumes that they will need to consume information similarly.

So what's different among these roles that you would need to cater for?

Table 3.2 Example Roles throughout the Organization

	Marketing	Sales	Development and Delivery	Human Resources	Information Technology	Finance and Audit	Executive and General Management
Strategic Management	CMO	EVP, sales	COO CDO VP, mfg	VP, HR	CTO CIO	CFO	CEO President
Operational Management	VP product mktg VP corp mktg VP direct mktg VP advertising VP corp communications	Regional VP, sales director, Sales ops	VP, product development VP prod mgt BU GM Director of quality assurance VP, R&D	HR directors Facilities director Director, learning and development	VP, end-user computing VP, security Director, software engineering Director, apps	VP, tax Director, finance Director, investor relations Controller Treasurer	Corp development VP, general counsel
Tactical Management	Product marketing managers	Sales directors	Engineering operations	HR managers	End user computing managers	Manager Financial Planning and Analysis (FPA), Director, budgeting	Special projects

The first difference in how information is needed by different roles is the intersection of dimensions. In Chapter 2, I talked about context and included items like product, customer, geography, and business unit (BU). A product manager for product X would generally be interested in information pertaining to product X, so the product dimension would be filtered for that product. For a sales manager, it might be by geography and customer type. So the public sector sales manager in California would only want to see sales numbers at the intersection of those two dimensions.

Another difference is in how the data is rolled up, also known as the data hierarchies. Finance would like numbers rolled up by cost center/profit center and business unit. Marketing would like numbers rolled up by customer segment, and product management would like numbers rolled up by product family. Yet all of these numbers have to tie-out at the top level.

In general terms, you can think of the three layers of the organization being interested or focused on different information domains as shown in Figure 3.2.

Strategic consumers of information generally want to see a unified view of information, aligned to strategic objectives. Operational types have more of a subject-matter focus, and tactical consumers go into detailed functional areas.

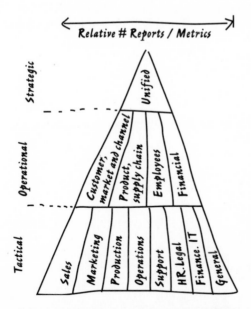

Figure 3.2   Volume and General Domain of Reports by Organization Level

Finally, different audiences generally consume information using different tools. This will be discussed further in the Enabling Technologies section of this chapter.

Information Qualities

When thinking about turning data into information, you have to consider all of the different qualities of that information. The following list is not exhaustive, but it's more complete than we usually get when planning how and when (and where) we gather our data and transform it into something people can use. This list is especially useful when designing business intelligence systems and planning on how to gather data and turn it into useable information.

Business Qualities of Information

- Accretion
- Dilution
- Velocity
- Risk weight
- Compounded annual growth rate (CAGR)
- Compliance: generally accepted accounting procedures (GAAP)/ International Financial Reporting Standards (IFRS)/Pro forma
- Financial statement impact: profit and loss, balance sheet, cash flow

Scenario Qualities of Information

- Actual
- Budget
- Forecast
- Plan: short-range, long-range, workforce, capital expenditure
- Benchmark
- Historic
- Variance
- Trends
- Outliers
- Seasonality
- Exceptions
- Benchmarks
- Sparseness/density
- Alerts

Contextual Qualities of Information

- Dimensionality
- Hierarchy (roll-up)

- Periodicity
- Refresh rate
- Granularity (level of detail)
- Version
- Currency (local, converted, triangulated)
- Time (fixed, year-to-date)
- Security, performance, dependence (tie-out)

Process Qualities of Information

- Goal setting
- Modeling
- Planning
- Monitoring
- Analyzing
- Reporting
- Collaboration

People Qualities of Information

- Ownership
- Role
- "Believe-ability"
- Contributor—they "read/write" information
- Consumer—they "read-only" information
- Executive sponsor

For example, if upper management says they want to focus and align on variable compensation, you would have to consider as many of the information qualities in the list as possible (or practical) to deliver a process and system that can become part of the EPM ecosystem. Some highlights would include:

- When is variable compensation reported—when it is accrued, earned, or disbursed (or all three)?
- Do we need to see variance between actual and planned variable comp?
- What level of detail do we need to drill down to—individual sales transactions for quota-carrying sales reps?
- Do we want to benchmark variable comp internally and externally?
- Who will consume this information? Will there be a workflow of approvals to track it?

Not everyone has the luxury to consider or investigate all of these qualities of information that they want to use in their EPM system. At least there has to be agreement on which qualities are most important to consider given your time and resource constraints.

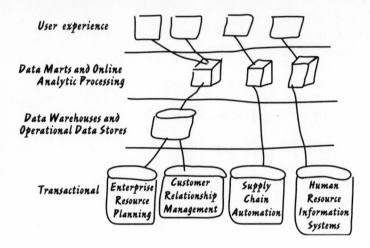

Figure 3.3   Generic Reporting Architecture

Information Delivery

In order to deliver the right information to the right people at the right time, it has to be gathered and transformed from the most granular transactional data, combined with related sources and presented in a useable way, based on your role and your purpose for consuming the information.

The traditional architecture of that flow is represented generically in Figure 3.3.

Data flows from the transactional sources at the bottom to reporting and analysis repository layers and on to front-end systems where users interact with the data.

Extract, transform, load (ETL) software is used to transport the data between layers.

Transactional Sources
- Mentioned in Chapter 1, in The Promise of EPM, these are where the day-to-day, minute-to-minute transactions are processed and stored.
- They are busy doing the real-time granular transactions throughout the business and deal primarily in "actuals"—not historical data, plans, forecasts, or what-if scenarios.

Data Warehouse, Operational Data Store
- The key transactional data is combined and warehoused in either an enterprise data warehouse (EDW) or, for select subject matters, a subject data warehouse, such as a sales data warehouse.

- An operational data store is usually a copy of the transactional data, duplicated in a repository to off-load reporting and analysis tasks from the transactional systems.
- In either a data warehouse or operational data store, you can add in plan and historical data.
- The goal is to off-load the burden of reporting, analysis, planning, and what-if modeling from the transactional systems so they can do what they do best and not get slowed down by the management operating system.

Data Marts

- Data marts, using online analytic processing (OLAP) technology (discussed in Chapter 4), are generally aggregations of the transactional data, and usually subject-matter specific.
- Data marts can be organized in a variety of different ways depending on your reporting requirements, including:
  - Financial statement: A P&L cube, a balance sheet cube, a cash-flow cube
  - Dimension: A product cube, a customer cube, an employee cube
  - Purpose: A reporting cube, a planning cube, a history cube

Consumption

Information is consumed by people. People have job roles or personae. The personae have unique points of view and key metrics they are concerned with. These metrics are used to help answer business questions or find new insights in order to sustainably execute their objectives—which, hopefully, are aligned with the company strategic objectives.

Typically, organizations are better at information delivery than they are at understanding and assisting in information consumption.

Notoriously low business intelligence (BI) system adoption rates support this observation: We can put out all the data and tools we want, but if managers aren't using them to make better decisions, so what?[1]

Two ways to improve information consumption are having the right tools and the right metrics in place to support users. Table 3.3 shows how typical BI tools are aligned with layers and roles in the organization.

There's more on metrics in Chapter 8. For now, during the Gather process of the management operating system, it's a good idea to tie metrics to roles.

The optimal number of metrics for each role is five to nine. The hard part is choosing the right five to nine.

Table 3.3 Matching the Tool to the Type of User

Layer in the Organization	Example Roles	Information Qualities	Typical BI Tools
Strategic	C-level (CEO, CFO, CIO, etc.) Executive or senior VP Managing director	■ Highly summarized ■ Monthly/quarterly ■ GAAP and non-GAAP ■ Static	■ Executive dashboard ■ Board-level book of reports ■ Consolidated management reports
Operational	VP Senior manager Manager	■ More detailed ■ Daily/weekly ■ Non-GAAP ■ Interactive ■ Cross-functional	■ Standard management reporting ■ Interactive query, analysis, and reporting (web-based)
Tactical	Line manager Back office Front lines (sales reps, customer support reps, etc.)	■ Very detailed ■ Near-real-time ■ Non-GAAP ■ Highly interactive ■ Function-focused	■ Spreadsheets ■ Interactive query, analysis, and reporting (web-based) ■ Purpose-built BI application (including mobile)

Here's a role-based way to apportion the five to nine metrics—for each intersection in the matrix in Table 3.3:

- two or three strategy metrics
- two or three function-wide metrics
- two or three intersection metrics

Role-based BI solutions would deliver the most important drivers of value in the business, from the perspective of where you live in the organization.

This gives focus, alignment, and accountability. Focus because it takes into account your organizational perspective (business function and layer), alignment by having visibility to your function's (department's) key drivers as well as the company strategy, and accountability because everyone up and down your branch of the organization chart can see your performance, and you are rewarded on your performance.

The metrics, of course, need to be the right mix of financial and operational, leading and lagging, tangible and intangible indicators, and need to follow a value-chain hierarchy so you can "drill down" into the details. I will say one thing about metrics prioritization: If you have too many to choose from, pick those that are most material (have the potential for the biggest financial impact on the business) and the most volatile (have the potential for the widest, fastest changes in the business).

Let's look at an example using a generic software company. Let's say their strategic objectives this year are 10% revenue growth, 20% operating margins, and improved year-over-year cash flow.

Using the organizational matrix from Table 3.3, what are the role-based metrics we would want delivered to Marketing Operations?

The strategic measures are: revenue growth, operating margin, and cash flow.

Some of the functional measures in marketing are: market share, net new customers, and average selling price (ASP).

Using a role-based selection method, the marketing operations dashboard, used by VPs in Marketing, would include:

- Revenue growth and margin (two strategy metrics)
- Market share, net new customers, and ASP (three function-wide metrics)
- Customer conversion, sales by product by geo, price discounts (three intersection metrics)

A particular focus on the last three can have a direct effect on the three function-wide metrics, which in turn can have a direct effect on revenue growth and margin (the two strategy metrics). For instance, success in customer conversions drives net new customers, which in turn drives revenue growth. More intelligent price discounts (or reduced discounts through better product marketing) drives ASP, which in turn drives margin.

Contribution

Most data is created at the transactional level; however, in EPM, much data can also be created in various management processes. This is especially true of enterprise planning. Here are some of the kinds of information that are generated by EPM systems and processes outside of transactional systems yet may write-back to a transactional system:

- Budgets, plans, forecasts, scenarios, and targets
- Statutory adjustments including intercompany eliminations, currency adjustments, reclassifications, and other journal entries
- Management overrides

- Audit adjustments (e.g., the difference between actual counted inventory and what the inventory management system says, due to shrinkage among other things)

Too much of this information is only captured and shared in spreadsheets. To store it in an enterprise system allows for better scrutiny, sharing and collaboration, auditability, and future reuse.

Classification

An important distinction to keep in mind while designing and building your management operating system is the classification of information and reports in the Gather process.

Classifying helps you assign the right process, tools, data, and resources to information, reports, and the Gather process. Without an overt classification, you can end up delivering information inefficiently, or worse, incorrectly.

Here are some common classifications:

- **Financial.** Usually relates to items found on the Profit and Loss statement, balance sheet, or cash flow. Content can be at a detailed or summary level.
- **Operational.** Usually contains information about volumes, units, headcount, inventory levels, and so on. Can also be at a detailed or summary level.
- **Executive.** Typically cross-functional information at a summary level.
- **Sustainability.** Information relating to environmental, health and safety, and community and social issues.
- **Management or Internal.** Includes flash reports. Typically contains information managers need to make business decisions before being transformed for external consumption.
- **Statutory or External.** Information that has been transformed according to GAAP or other regulatory standards.
- **Canned.** Standard reports that are used over and over again.
- **Ad Hoc.** Usually one-time information that's situational and does not need to be retrieved later—although if found useful across different audiences and at different times can quickly find its way into a canned report.

Management and Statutory Reporting

The majority of the Gathering process—financial and operational monitoring, reporting, and alerting—is done in aid of internal management of the

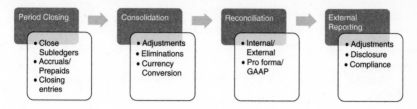

Figure 3.4   End-to-End Financial Close Process at a High Level

business. There is a requirement for external reporting, primarily for publicly traded companies, but also for government organizations, privately owned companies (regulatory and bank reporting for example), nonprofits, and other organizations.

In order to do this external reporting, there has to be a well-defined process in place that occurs monthly, quarterly, and annually. This process is called the financial "close" process or "closing the books" and includes the steps shown in Figure 3.4.

Financial Consolidation

Most organizations have more than one financial source system such as an enterprise resource planning (ERP) or general ledger (GL) program. The larger the organization is, or the more geographically dispersed, or more active in mergers and acquisitions, the more ERP and GL systems they have.

At some point, the financial data from all entities in an organization have to be consolidated to create a company-wide "top-level" financial view that can be analyzed and reported. For externally reported financial data, additional transformations take place at the aggregated level to comply with government and regulatory standards. At some point, foreign currencies have to be converted into a standard currency or constant dollar. Surprisingly, many organizations still do this consolidation in Excel or back in the ERP or GL systems. This quickly gives rise to problems in transparency, auditability, controls, and governance. The rise of purpose-built, comprehensive financial consolidation and reporting management systems is primarily due to addressing these problems as well as the increased demand for additional controls and regulations—like Sarbanes-Oxley in the United States and IFRS internationally.

Alternate Hierarchies

In order to combine this external or statutory look at the business with the way management looks at the business to do internal reporting and make management decisions, these purpose-built consolidation systems generally support multiple, simultaneous roll-ups or hierarchies. This is done without having to reload the data from source systems for each "look" at the business.

Some of the ways managers want to look at the business differently, include:

- By legal entity
- By organizational BU or segment
  - A segment can be a territory, division, department, or even product category
- Geographically for all products, all BUs (looking for territory effectiveness)
- By product category for all geographies across all BUs (looking for cross-sell effectiveness)
- By cost center for all BUs (looking for shared-service opportunities)
- Or by accounting treatment
  - US GAAP
  - Local GAAP
  - IFRS
  - Pro forma

Allocations

The transformation of information at the top level of the business typically includes a variety of allocations, including the allocation of indirect costs, such as overhead costs, to business units or product lines. Let's say you were interested in reporting on BU profitability, yet all your business units used the same shared services center including HR, Legal, Procurement, and IT. How do you allocate the costs for those services back to each business unit? There are a variety of allocation methodologies, including by:

- Revenue produced by each group
- Headcount of each group
- Square footage occupied by each group

Or some combination of these methodologies and your own method unique to your business.

There are two points to be made about allocations when doing EPM right. One is that the methodology selected must be fair, transparent, and consistently applied for there to be buy-in across all business units and functions. As long as there is agreement and people understand they are being allocated costs fairly, there is more chance of success of those people buying in to the numbers. The other is that your EPM system must automatically do the allocation for you, based on the methodology you choose, and, ideally, help you select the right methodology by modeling all relevant combinations during the period of enrolling and debating with business units and functions on getting agreement on what constitutes fair.

Another kind of allocation that EPM systems help with is the spreading of numbers collected at one level into a more granular level. For example, to calculate weekly profitability where you collect daily revenue amounts, weekly direct expenses, and monthly overhead expenses, you would roll up the daily revenue to a week, apply the weekly direct expenses, and then spread the monthly overheads back into each week based on the percentage of revenue contained in each week. This isn't always perfect, but if applied consistently, it can be useful for comparing prior periods, understanding seasonality, and other insights.

If the reporting, consolidation, allocations, and spreads are all done within an EPM process and as part of a management operating system, there will be better shared accountability, shared understanding, and shared focus.

Sustainability Reporting

As demands for more corporate transparency and concerns for environmental and social responsibilities increase, more organizations are publishing publicly available sustainability reports.

These reports help show the organization's impact on a variety of areas including:

The Environment
- Greenhouse gas emissions
- Waste production and management
- Water usage
- Energy consumption

Employee Well-Being
- Health
- Safety
- Working conditions
- Skills and Training

Social Responsibility
- Community impact
- Charitable giving
- Compliance

In North America, sustainability reporting is not mandated by the government, so organizations voluntarily choose to produce this kind of information. However, companies are discovering that it makes good business sense to be transparent in these areas as customers and consumers regularly make buying decisions based on sustainability criteria, as do "socially responsible" investors. Most of my Fortune 500 clients produce some sort of corporate social responsibility report in their annual report. In the rest of the world, sustainability or "integrated reporting" itself, or elements of it, is becoming mandatory. For example, in the United Kingdom by 2013, all companies listed on the London Stock Exchange (about 1,600 companies) will be required to report their greenhouse gas emissions.

As this is a newer area of corporate reporting, unlike financial reporting, there are relatively fewer reporting standards and requirements. The most common format, from the Global Reporting Initiative, or GRI, has been adopted by many hundreds of companies and will likely be the de facto standard globally.

The GRI also provides almost one hundred key performance indicators for sustainability reporting, organized in the following categories:

Economic
- Economic performance
- Market presence
- Indirect economic impacts

Environmental
- Materials
- Energy
- Water
- Biodiversity
- Emissions, effluents, and waste
- Products and services
- Compliance
- Transport

Societal Performance: Labor Practices and Decent Work
- Employment
- Labor/management relations

- Occupational health and safety
- Training and education
- Diversity and equal opportunity

Societal Performance: Human Rights

- Investment and procurement practices
- Nondiscrimination
- Freedom of association and collective bargaining
- Child labor
- Forced and compulsory labor
- Security policies
- Indigenous rights

Social Performance: Society

- Community
- Corruption
- Public policy
- Anticompetitive behavior
- Compliance

Social Performance: Product Responsibility

- Customer health and safety
- Products and services labeling
- Marketing communications
- Customer privacy
- Compliance

Since 2000, the United Nations Global Compact has been tracking organizations that participate in publicly reporting their sustainability initiatives and outcomes. There are over 6,000 businesses worldwide who participate.

Some of the best examples of sustainability reporting come from these companies:

- Nike
- BMW
- BASF
- Nestlé
- Ericsson
- BT
- AEP

One of the challenges of good sustainability reporting has been data quality. Companies have not typically measured many of the transactional

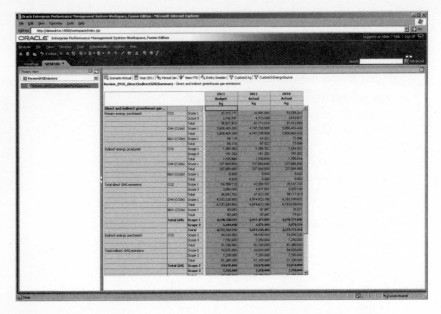

Figure 3.5   Sustainability Reporting in Oracle Hyperion Financial Management
Courtesy of Oracle Corp.

elements that are found in the GRI categories listed. However, once they have measured or derived actuals, there are a variety of EPM systems available to report, as shown in Figure 3.5.

The next generation of corporate social responsibility and sustainability is called "shared value" as described by Michael Porter and Mark Kramer.[2] It promotes:

- Joint company and community value creation
- Improving economic and societal benefits relative to cost
- Using social and environmental responsibility as a competitive differentiator
- Contributing to the "triple bottom line" (integrated reporting on people, planet, and profit)

Just as you would include financial and operational drivers and processes in the management operating system to create real enterprise performance management, you can include all of the components of sustainability reporting in your models, plans, forecasts, reports, and analyses. In fact, corporate social responsibility and creating shared value will be as important as financial

Group Highlights

Highlights

ⓘ More information on our operations on page 48   ⓘ More information on our corporate responsibility activities on page 38

Operational highlights

– Initial £100m strategic investment programme within target range – overall
  annualised post tax return of 12.2% for projects which are fully up and running
– Next phase £150m strategic investment programme on track
– The UK business delivered 6% revenue growth and UK Municipal PFI/PPP
  contracts achieved 10% trading margins up from 6.4% last year
– The Organics business across all our markets delivered 28% revenue growth
  and trading margins increased from 13% to 18%
– Another strong performance from our Dutch Hazardous Waste business
  with trading profit up 26% in the year

Financial highlights

– Robust performance in challenging trading conditions
– Underlying profit before tax up 8% at constant currency
– Management actions delivered £11m of cost savings to offset challenging market
  conditions in our Solid Waste businesses
– Strong cash generation with underlying free cash-flow conversion at 81%
– Net debt to EBITDA ratio of 1.7 times versus our target of below 2.5 times
  and covenant of 3.0 times

Corporate responsibility highlights

– Reportable accident rate improved by 13%
– Overall recycling and recovery rate up to 78% from 77% last year
– 1.28 million tonnes of carbon avoided
– Local neighbourhood complaints fell by 32%

Figure 3.6   Shanks Group Plc 2012 Annual Report Page 1
Source: Shanks Group Plc

and operational results for investors, customers, partners, and employees, as the first page of Shanks Group Plc 2012 annual report shown in
Figure 3.6 illustrates.

Enabling Technologies

The goals of the Gather process of the management cycle are not just
to spit out reports. They include transforming data into useful, actionable
information and delivering it to the right person at the right time. This
takes more than reporting tools. It also takes data management tools, data
integration and transformation tools, monitoring and alerting, and so on. The
typical high-level structure looks like Figure 3.7, with the data at the bottom,
being transformed and managed in the middle, and delivered to users at the

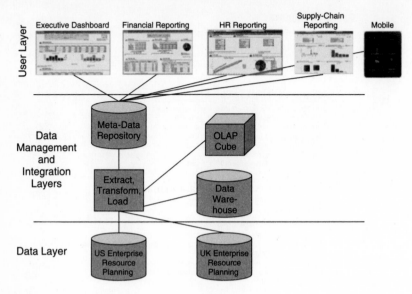

Figure 3.7   Typical Reporting High-level Architecture

top. Obviously it's a lot more complex than that in real life, but generally the layers are the same.

There are a lot of "front-end" or user-experience tools you can use. You probably use more of them in your organization than you know about. In one EPM requirements client engagement, after interviewing multiple finance and business-unit stakeholders, we uncovered thirteen reporting tools that IT did not know about. And spreadsheets, while great for quick ad hoc reporting and analysis, are not meant to be an enterprise reporting tool.

Other tools used at the front end to deliver the information include:

- Executive dashboards
- Data visualization
- Scorecards
- Board-level books
- Consolidated management reports
- Flash reports
- Functional management reports
- Interactive query and reporting

- Spreadsheets
- Purpose-built applications

Tools used in the data management and integration layers include:

- Alerting
- Semantic layer
- An OLAP engine
- In-memory databases
- ETL
- Data quality
- Master data management, meta-data management
- Mobile platform

Rationalization

With the abundance of unused, and frankly useless, reports in any organization, and with the advances in information management and reporting tools, many companies are embarking on a reporting rationalization program. There are at least three ways of doing this. One is from the bottom up. By going throughout the organization and taking an inventory of what reporting processes and systems there are, and capturing what reports are out there (using a classification system like that presented earlier in this chapter), under the "Classification" heading, organizations can understand the entire scope of reporting and begin to identify duplicative processes, redundant systems, and unused reports. They can standardize the process of gathering data into information and consuming it, consolidate front-end and data management systems, and rationalize which reports are needed and which can be discarded. Another way to do this is from the top down. By starting with strategic objectives and key value drivers (more on this in Chapter 8), companies can align systems, processes and information to those that support business requirements. And the third way is to do both—find out what you have, find out what you need, and add what's missing, delete what's not needed, and make changes to what's close.

As you unify solutions to support the Gather process, there should be emphasis and priority placed on self-serve reporting and the ability to accommodate changing data, metadata, and delivery methods. As with most initiatives today, you have to remain flexible, adaptive, and cost-effective.

Potential Quick Wins

Many vendors produce out-of-the-box information dashboards that connect directly to your source systems through standard mappings from metrics on the dashboard to data elements in the transactional systems. With minimal configuration and tailoring, these solutions can quickly present the information you have and highlight your gaps.

One way to get started is by doing a functional value map of the organization, or a subset, to show how information is connected, what drivers are important, and how it all interconnects. See Chapter 8 for more information.

A scorecard is like a business checklist: put all the KPIs, financial and nonfinancial, in one place so you can check off where you are: Revenue growth, check. Gross margin, check. Operating margin, check. And so on. These are still popular at the executive level and help garner support for EPM initiatives.

However, the Gather architecture cannot be designed and built in isolation. It has to live with and integrate to the other components of EPM as we will see in the next three chapters and finally in Chapter 9, Bringing It All Together.

Summary

The Gather process is a key part of the EPM management operating system, and some say it's the starting place, since it answers the question "Where are we right now?" It is designed to take all of the detailed data (scattered throughout the organization) we have, gather it, and turn it into meaningful information from which we can get new insights and begin to make better decisions.

So how is getting better at the Gather process a competitive advantage? Ideally, it improves your decision reaction time by letting people spend more time on doing more with the numbers than collecting, massaging, and proving the numbers. It improves confidence in the numbers since there is transparency on where they came from and how they were transformed (not from a mysterious spreadsheet). It supports making fact-based decisions since the numbers are based in reality—you still may need analyses to help with the decisions, but you know those are populated with the same numbers you looked at to find out where you are. With better access to relevant information, showing where the numbers come from and being able to drill down into the details, and how what people are working on is connected to overall company objectives, financial literacy can improve in all areas of the organization. Imagine giving all employees the ability to behave like owners!

You may have everything you need at this point to take some action. The next steps may be quite obvious, as with a wide variance to target with a correlated cause—like one sales team is missing their sales targets for three months in-a-row while every other sales team is meeting theirs, and this particular sales team has an open headcount for the sales team manager.

However, the reason you got the results you got, may not be that obvious. EPM can help you understand why.

Notes

1. Mark Smith, Ventana Research, "The Pathetic State of Dashboards," August 2012.
2. Michael Porter and Mark Kramer, "Creating Shared Value," *Harvard Business Review*, January–February 2011.

CHAPTER 4

Understand: Turning Insights into Actions

To understand is to perceive patterns.

—Sir Isaiah Berlin

What is the next step once you have all the data you need that not only suits your role and your tasks at hand, but is also a good reflection of reality? Understanding why you got the results you did can potentially help you avoid them (if they're negative) or help you duplicate them (if they're positive) in the future.

If we look at the Understand process within the management operating system in more detail, as in Figure 4.1, we see:

- **Drill down.** Consumers of all that information will want to drill down into the details.
- **Point of View (POV).** When users "slice-and-dice" the data, they create a specific point of view. They look at specific products, by customers, for certain time periods, compared to historical information. And when they want additional reporting on their findings, they want that specific point of view passed on to the Gather process.
- **Financial and Operational Analytics.** Including trending, benchmarking, outliers, ratios, ranking, and visualization.
- **Facts.** Facts uncovered in the Understand process can be fed into the models within the Debate process.
- **Predictions.** When a what-if scenario is developed, you want to analyze the probabilities of various predictions to see which is the most likely to occur.
- **Adjust.** Using findings from the Understand process, you may want to revise some strategies or strategic targets.
- **Validate.** You use the Understand process to help validate strategic objectives.

Figure 4.1   Close-Up of the Understand Process, and Its Inputs and Outputs

Business Questions

The usual starting place for trying to understand all that information is a desire to answer a business question.

There are four foundational—or "starting" questions—as described in Chapter 2:

1. Where are we right now compared to where we said we would be?
2. Why did we get what we got? What happened to give us those results?
3. What do we want to happen? What is possible in our industry, in this economy? And what's next?
4. How will we get it done? Who will do what, and by when?

These questions help us align our strategy, objectives, and initiatives with our intended results. They help challenge our objectives and help generate and reveal our assumptions, constraints, and value drivers. The answers to these questions should validate our financial and operational targets.

Some typical business questions include:

- "Who are my top 20 customers and what are they buying this quarter?"
- "Are my sales people on track to meet quota?"
- "Why is it taking so long to fill open headcount?"
- "Which marketing campaigns are generating the most leads?"
- "What's the conversion ratio (from lead to sale) compared to last year?"
- "What's the current customer attrition rate, and top reasons for leaving?"
- "Are products being delivered on time? Do we have the right balance of inventory levels?"

- "What percentage of sales is coming from new products? Is this a good measure of innovation?"
- "What's our forecast accuracy, and when will it surpass the threshold of reliability?"
- "How are raw material prices trending by region?"

There are an infinite number of questions. Some are the same week over week, month over month, and some are needed only for a specific area of concern until a problem is solved.

Business questions help break silos—to answer most of them, you'll have to incorporate both financial and operational data and information from a variety of business functions like Sales, Marketing, Operations, HR, Finance, and so on. The questions are generally forward looking, yet they need information from the past (although "past performance is not a guarantee of future results.") Managers generally need some analytics in order to know what to ask (or the right questions to ask). The answers to business questions should help drive actions.

Let's take the example of sales forecasts and walk them through the four questions to illustrate how important it is to understand why you got the results you got. Say you had a total sales plan—across all regions, channels, and products—for this quarter of $1 million. It's the end of the second month in the quarter, so you would expect to currently be at $666,666 of actual sales with a remaining forecast of $333,334. (By the way, it doesn't really work this way—rarely are sales results distributed that evenly across a quarter and rarely, if ever, does the sales forecast match the gap in the plan!) You gather all of the sales actual data from your contract system and all of the forecast data from your customer relationship management (CRM) or sales forecasting system. Your actual sales figure at this point is $500,000 and your forecast for the rest of the quarter is $300,000. Immediately you see that you will have a shortfall for the quarter of $200,000 unless something happens, probably something drastic, in the last month of the quarter. This answers the first question: "Where are we compared to where we said we would be?" You could spring into action at this point and have all of your sales managers read the riot act to each sales rep and insist on a revised (upwards) forecast and that everyone pull out all the stops on selling to make up the potential shortfall. Or you could ask the question "why?"

When you ask why, you have to know something about how the information you have is organized. The easiest organizing principal is the hierarchy of the data, or how it is rolled up from each sales rep, through sales managers, to regions and finally to the top number—which is where you noticed the shortfall in the first place. To get into the details of the forecast, you would "drill down" into the hierarchy. Let's say you drill down into each region and when you compare region to region, you notice that their quarter-to-date actuals plus forecasted amounts are all off by about 20% from the plan for each region. So no one region sticks out from the others as an anomaly, or the cause of the shortfall. However, your forecast data also has a product hierarchy since each rep forecasts sales by product. When you then drill down into the product forecast you notice each product-family forecast is fairly close to the plan except one: It's 75% off of plan. You further drill down into that product family and find one product with very low actual sales quarter-to-date and almost none forecast for the rest of the quarter. Let's say that product is "Consulting Services," something you try to sell with every product sale as a way for customers to implement what you're selling them. If your sales forecasting system captures such information, you could drill down right into the forecast itself and see what reason codes were given for losing the sale of Consulting Services to try and understand the root cause. If it doesn't, you can call a few sales managers to find out what's going on. Let's say that what you find is that customers are unhappy with the skills and availability of your consultants and choose to self-implement or find help elsewhere.

At this point, you have found your root cause of the shortfall and you understand why you got what you got. But we're not done. What are you going to do about it? You confer with the senior sales and product manager and you brainstorm possible actions to take, and you come up with:

- Deeply discount consulting services rates to get consultants off the bench and try and make-up the shortfall with volume.
- Increase product prices or remove discounts for the last month of the quarter.
- Go back to all the customers in the pipeline and try to up-sell and cross-sell product to make up the difference.
- Go into those secondary markets you have been avoiding and try and get some net new customers by the end of the quarter.
- Work with your channel partners, deliver some rapid product training, and engage them to perform the implementation services (and to mark up their fees to help make up the shortfall).

What's the best action to take? It depends on which course of action gives us the best chance of making our number by the end of the quarter (one of our desired results), yet not at the risk of upsetting the other desired results of the business, including customer satisfaction, repeat sales, reference-able customers, gross margin attainment, and so on. The second part of Understand is to determine what's next, which is going to require an EPM-supported debate. I'll come back to this in Chapter 5.

Root Cause

For now, let's look at how we use analytics to help us understand the root cause of a result. Referring back to Table 2.1, the business function and layer matrix, a useful way to look at root cause is by using the business matrix and metric decomposition. Using the previous example, it might look like Figure 4.2.

Each business driver can be related to one or more drivers in different areas of the business. For example, good quality consulting drives marketing references that help make new sales. The relationships show paths to possible root causes.

If we were not getting the desired level or quantity of references, we would look into the following for possible root causes:

- Consulting quality
- Consultant availability
- Consulting rates

To do the root cause analysis, we'll need to be able to drill in to the details of the data. For this, we'll need the data to be related through a hierarchy structure. But before we jump into hierarchy, it's interesting to notice in Figure 4.2 just how many connections come into and out of References—it

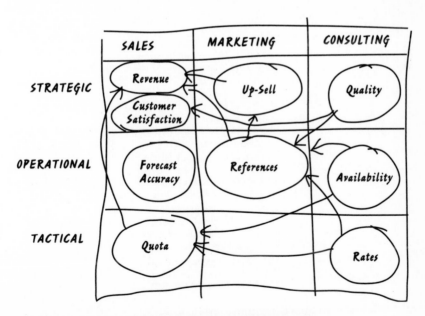

Figure 4.2   Metric Decomposition within the Business Matrix

could be a key value driver. So the question to ask is, "Are we reporting, analyzing, modeling and planning references?"

Multidimensional Cubes

In Chapter 2, I talked about the context of information and how important it is to EPM. This context, the intersection of all the "dimensions" of a piece of data, is stored along with the data in a special database called a multidimensional database, sometimes referred to as a "cube." The technology behind multidimensional databases, called online analytic processing (OLAP), is distinguished from regular transactional databases (like those used in your ERP, G/L, Supply Chain Management [SCM], CRM, and other systems) because it inherently aggregates data using a predefined hierarchy or roll-up structure as shown in Figure 4.3.

The major benefit of the cube is that data is always aggregated and "pre-calculated," meaning the sums (and products and other formulae) are already applied at all levels of the hierarchy. When you drill down into the details, the results are ready and waiting.

Having a business question and knowing the drill-path are good starting places; however, you need more than that for understanding why you got your results.

```
Product
    100 (+) (Alias: Colas)
        100-10 (+) (Alias: Cola)
        100-20 (+) (Alias: Diet Cola)
        100-30 (+) (Alias: Caffeine Free Cola)
    200 (+) (Alias: Root Beer)
        200-10 (+) (Alias: Old Fashioned)
        200-20 (+) (Alias: Diet Root Beer)
        200-30 (+) (Alias: Sasparilla)
        200-40 (+) (Alias: Binch Beer)
    300 (+) (Alias: Cream Soda)
        300-10 (+) (Alias: Dark Cream)
        300-20 (+) (Alias: Vanilla Cream)
        300-30 (+) (Alias: Diet Cream)
    400 (+) (Alias: Fruit Soda)
        400-10 (+) (Alias: Grape)
        400-20 (+) (Alias: Orange)
        400-30 (+) (Alias: Strawberry)
    Diet (~) (Alias: Diet Drinks)
        100-20 (+) (Shared Member)
        200-20 (+) (Shared Member)
        300-30 (+) (Shared Member)
```

Figure 4.3   Sample Roll-Up in an OLAP Database

Patterns and New Insights

There are things you already know about your industry, about your business, about your customers and employees. And there are things that, if you don't know them, you know how to find out. It's those things that you didn't even know existed that are the most interesting insights. One way to uncover those new insights is through the detection of patterns.

Patterns

A pattern can help us see the cause and effect relationship either directly or indirectly. They can also cause us to ask more questions, and that's fine, so long as those next questions lead on a path of discovery that gets you closer to your answer. Let's take a look at fourteen common analytic patterns and how they help us learn and discover root cause.

Pattern 1: Time-Series

Probably the most common analyses done in EPM systems, because of their roots in Finance, are time-series analyses. This is where information is presented month by month, quarter by quarter, and year by year. Sometimes they show monthly discrete totals and sometimes accumulated year- or quarter-to-date totals, like the Income Statement in Figure 4.4.

Madelyn's Biscuits

Income Statement
For the Period Ended May 31, 2011

	January	February	March	Q1	April	May	QTD	YTD
Revenue								
Sales	$ 40,100	$ 43,500	$ 52,100	$ 135,700	$ 57,881	$ 60,775	$ 118,657	$ 254,357
Sales Returns	-	-	1,200.00	1,200.00	-	750.00	750.00	1,950.00
Sales Discounts	2,200	4,100	5,513	11,813	2,900	3,510	6,410	18,223
Net Sales	$ 42,300	$ 47,600	$ 58,813	$ 148,713	$ 60,781	$ 65,035	$ 125,817	$ 274,529
Cost of Goods Sold	$ 20,000	$ 21,000	$ 22,050	$ 63,050	$ 23,153	$ 24,310	$ 47,463	$ 110,513
Gross Profit	$ 22,300	$ 26,600	$ 36,763	$ 85,663	$ 37,629	$ 40,725	$ 78,354	$ 164,016
Operating Expenses				$ -			$ -	$ -
Salaries & Wages	$ 9,200	$ 9,200	$ 9,800	$ 28,200	$ 9,200	$ 9,116	$ 18,316	$ 46,516
Depreciation Expenses	650	525	520	1,695	509	616	1,125	2,820
Office Expenses	300	500	600	1,400	330	540	870	2,270
Rent Expense	1,750	1,750	1,750	5,250	1,750	1,750	3,500	8,750
Travel Expenses	1,290	-	800	2,090	-	2,100	2,100	4,190
Maintenance Expenses	350	1,200	1,010	2,560	300	560	860	3,420
Marketing Expenses	1,200	560	342	2,102	400	600	1,000	3,102
Total Operating Expense	$ 14,740	$ 13,735	$ 14,822	$ 43,297	$ 12,489	$ 15,282	$ 27,771	$ 71,068
Income From Operation	$ 7,560	$ 12,865	$ 21,941	$ 42,366	$ 25,140	$ 25,443	$ 50,583	$ 92,948
Interest Income (Expense)	(100)	(105)	(110)	(315)	(116)	(122)	(237)	(553)
Income Before Income T	$ 7,460	$ 12,760	$ 21,830	$ 42,050	$ 25,024	$ 25,321	$ 50,345	$ 92,396
Income Tax Expense	750	788	827	2,364	868	912	1,780	4,144
Net Incom	$ 6,710	$ 11,973	$ 21,003	$ 39,686	$ 24,156	$ 24,410	$ 48,565	$ 88,251

Figure 4.4   Standard Time Series Financial Report

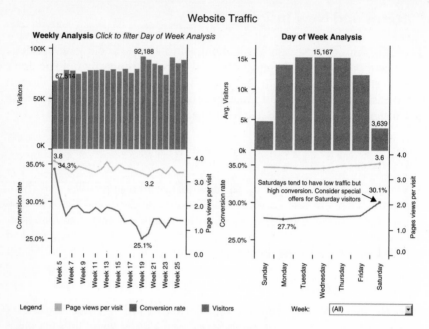

Figure 4.5   Example of Multivariate and Comparison Patterns
Courtesy Tableau Software Inc.

Pattern 2: Multivariate

Organizations are complex, so visualizing and consuming information using more than two variables is necessary. In Figure 4.5, you can see how conversion rates and page views vary with the number of visitors and week number (left-hand side), and how conversion rates vary with day of week (right-hand side) and one possible test to deploy based on this insight.

Pattern 3: Comparison

Any dimension or variable can be compared: Current period to prior period, to prior year, to history beyond prior year; actual to forecast, actual to plan, actual to budget; Product 1 to Product 2; Region 1 to Region 2; and so on. Also see Pattern 13, Variance Analysis—which is generally what you look at when you compare things.

Pattern 4: Distribution

How your data deviates from normal distribution patterns can give you insights into where to look for the root cause of problems or anomalies. For example, in Figure 4.6, we quickly see that there is a very high number of records (transactions) that have a $100 loss.

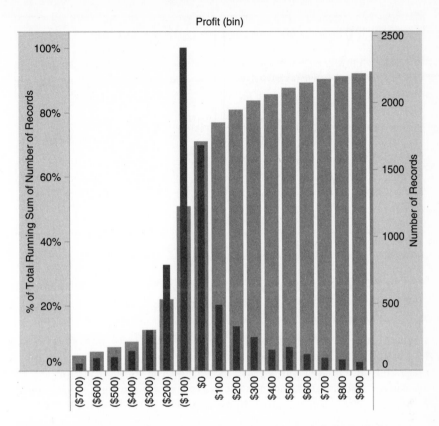

Figure 4.6   Distribution of Each Record that Falls within Each $100 Profit Range
Courtesy Tableau Software Inc.

Pattern 5: From–To

On its own, a path between two points is usually uninformative. However, when a collection of from and to points is plotted relatively to a central starting point, or in combination with other from–to data, like those shown in Figure 4.7, interesting patterns can emerge.

Pattern 6: Rankings

Ranking quickly give you possible areas of focus (e.g., top 20 or bottom 20 customers or regions). Also interesting are changes in ranking from a prior period. If your number-one-selling product moves to number two next month, and number four the following month, that's a pattern worth investigating.

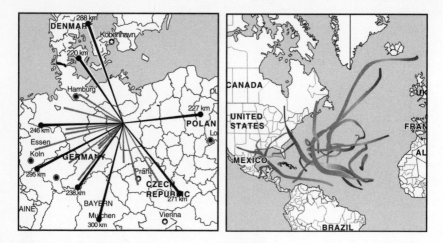

Figure 4.7   From–To Patterns: Deliveries Out of Berlin (Left), Gulf Coast Hurricanes (Right)
Courtesy Tableau Software Inc.

Pattern 7: Outliers and Deviation

Looking at data that falls outside the norm can yield new insights. In Figure 4.8, for that one data point on the far right, how did we get so much program from a relatively modest size sale? How can we duplicate that success elsewhere? And for that one point at the top, why did we get so little profit from such a large sale, and how can we avoid that in the future?

Pattern 8: Trends

Although past performance is no guarantee of future results, we can still learn from our historical data. You have to know if the best fit of a trend line will be linear, logarithmic, or polynomial. For example, logarithmic trends may be better for analyzing data over long time periods.

The richness of trends depends partly on how much historical data you keep online (available for analysis). How much data to keep, and at what level of detail, is different for each organization and is dictated by statutory requirements for some. Figure 4.9 shows a variety of trend lines along with their polynomial fit for average discounts received from four suppliers over the last four years.

Pattern 9: Correlation

Correlation is the degree to which two or more quantities are linearly associated. Remember correlation does not equal causation, and it's important to know what could "move the needle."

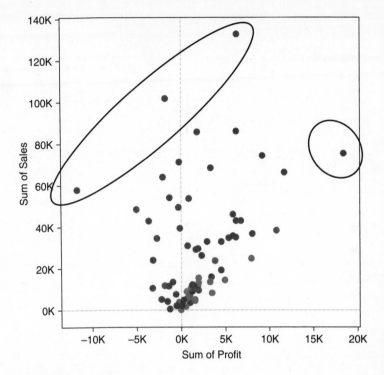

Figure 4.8   Outliers
Courtesy Tableau Software Inc.

For example, in Figure 4.10 you can see a correlation between a customer's age and the amount of money they spend in a transaction. To determine if there is a particular price point that is attractive to a customer demographic, you can test this hypothesis by altering prices, measuring results, and looking for the correlation. See Chapter 5 for more on testing.

Pattern 10: Clustering

Clustering is a way to group data with common characteristics. For example, in Figure 4.10, we see three distinct groups of customers based on age and amount purchased. You could use this kind of clustering pattern to help inform product pricing and promotions—to help target products to the purchasing trends of various demographics.

Pattern 11: Segmentation

Segmentation, like clustering, is dividing a group into smaller parts based on declared criteria.

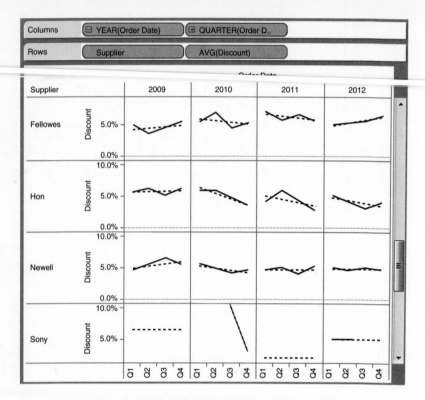

Figure 4.9   Multiple Trend Lines: Discount by Quarter/Year by Supplier
Courtesy Tableau Software Inc.

Most often, this grouping is done around customers and markets. Market segmentation can be geographical (West, Central, East), company size (enterprise, midsize, small business), company type (commercial, higher-ed, public sector), industry (financial services, manufacturing, retail), or other criteria that match your business objectives. Customer segmentation can include demographics (age, income, gender), buying patterns (repeat, one-time, early-adopter), or, again, any criteria that you determine helps analyze your business. Segmentation gives you another dimension to markets or customers that lets you drill into and look for patterns and new insights.

Pattern 12: Geospatial

Seeing results displayed in their geography can give new insights about markets, logistics, demographics, and so on. In Figure 4.11, you see a high concentration of bicycle collisions at a certain intersection and you can take action as a result—erect additional signage for example.

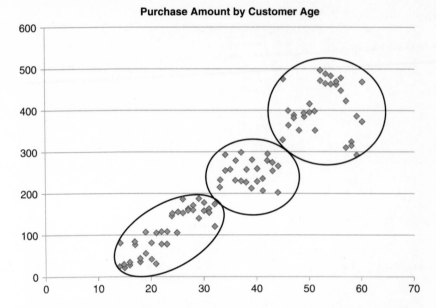

Figure 4.10   Dollar Purchase Amounts versus Customer Age Shows Three Distinct Buying Clusters

Pattern 13: Variance Analysis

You can analyze many kinds of variance:

- Actuals versus plan and forecast
- Actuals versus prior period (prior year, month, quarter)
- Same product line, one geography versus another (for actuals versus plan and/or actuals versus prior period)
- Variance among scenarios, and so on

A good way to report the cause of a variance is using a waterfall chart, also known as a bridge chart, walk-chart, or causal chart. It shows the net additions and subtractions (amounts and reasons) to account for the total variance between one number and another. For example, in Figure 4.12, we see a causal chart showing the variance in trading profit from prior year (2011) to current year (2012) for Shanks Plc in the United Kingdom.

Like any good analysis or report, this chart tells a story. I like this example because it attributes most of the potential losses to the Market and most of the profit to Management Actions and Strategy—the folks at Shanks look like heroes!

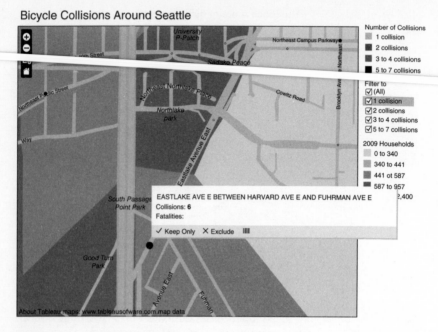

Figure 4.11   Geospatial Example
Courtesy Tableau Software Inc.

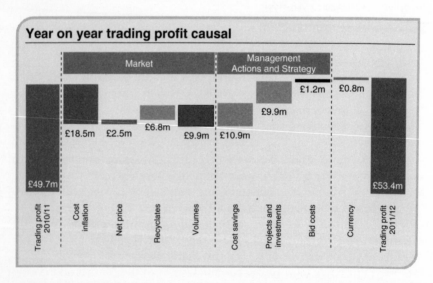

Figure 4.12   Waterfall Chart
Source: Shanks PLC Annual Report and Accounts, 2012

Pattern 14: Benchmarks (internal and external)

Some businesses used to rely on external benchmarks to help gauge the effectiveness of their operations and results. The thinking was that, within an industry, there was only so much operating margin to attain, or that the key financial ratios had to be within certain upper and lower limits. While popular in the last ten years, this attitude or approach has changed. During times of high growth, companies would ask why these limits were there and who was to say our unique business model could break those limits? And during times of low or no growth, companies would notice that the game had changed and that new business models were necessary for survival.

Today, many of my clients discredit external benchmarks and don't want to compare themselves to the competition (external benchmarks). They would rather compare themselves across business units (internal benchmarks) or outside of their industries (so-called "best practices"), or not benchmark at all.

Enrollment

An often-overlooked EPM skill is being able to communicate what the data, information, and analyses mean. Using the "story" of the data, as mentioned earlier, is a way to enroll other people in your insight or conclusion. Surely you'll have defensible facts on your side, however sometimes it requires an emotional appeal and some passion[1] to persuade your listeners enough to give what you're saying enough priority to take action above all the other priorities they have.

Big Data and Predictive Analytics

To address the sometimes overwhelming volume, frequency, complexity, and potential impact of new data, we needed a new way to describe it. The term "Big Data" was coined to differentiate the profusion of unstructured data, social media data, machine-generated data, and so on from the "regular" data that has been generated by transactional systems for years. The term wasn't coined just to describe the volume of data, but also the impact it will have. This will be big. Erik Brynjolfsson and Andrew McAfee say Big Data has the potential to revolutionize management.[2]

Structuring Unstructured Data

The first challenge of harnessing all that Big Data is to gather it and transform it into meaningful insights. So you have to structure the unstructured. This is done using a variety of approaches and proprietary "engines" that work on

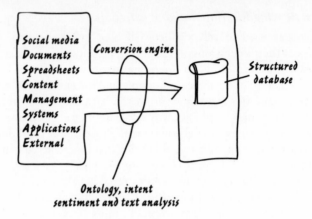

Figure 4.13   Structuring Unstructured Data

deciphering the meaning of unstructured data and depositing it into subject matter areas such as customer, product, company, market, employee, and so on. Figure 4.13 shows the typical flow of data from unstructured to structured by way of a "black box" that contains the algorithms that transform the data. On the other side of the transformation, the data becomes just another source that can be used like any other data source—for reporting (Gather), analytics (Understand), modeling (Debate), and planning (Commit) in the management operating system.

Some Big Data use cases include those shown in Table 4.1.

Predictive Analytics

Predictive analytics is the part of EPM that deals with extracting patterns from historical data and using them to predict possible future trends and patterns. The accuracy of a prediction is dependent on how well the drivers, constraints, and assumptions have been captured and used in the prediction.

While no one can predict the future with complete certainty or accuracy, ranges of probability can be useful to govern resource deployment decisions and expectations-setting. There are a variety of statistical techniques and algorithms that can be used against the historical data you have, and the one that works for your particular analysis is the one that comes closest to what actually happens. So, again, another opportunity for testing using EPM: Apply several methodologies for a predictive analysis, measure actual results, and compare. Repeat to see if the closest methodology stands up over time and over varying market conditions.

For example, Proctor & Gamble has a Business Sufficiency program that gives insights about market share and other KPIs for up to 12 months in the

Table 4.1 Big Data Use Cases

Unstructured Data	Structured Data	Use Case
Twitter feeds mentioning your company's customer service	Net promoter score (NPS)	Alerting to any surge (positive or negative) in NPS and correlated to an event (like a product launch) can let customer service management take actions to address root causes
Facebook comments and Likes for a particular product in a particular geography	Product demand forecast	Possible immediate up-stock of specific products in specific regions/stores for short-term burst of sales
A surge in documents created on users' computers with the word "resume" in the file name or content	Employee satisfaction index	Understand root cause to prevent a surge in unwanted attrition
Multiple sources (twitter, blogs, news feeds) citing impending rise in fuel prices	Commodity cost forecast	Revise time to deliver models Revise price models Adjust fuel hedge
Real-time usage data is being captured on who is using which EPM reports and when	Usage patterns by report	Retire unused reports Provision IT infrastructure to support peak demand Provide additional training for reports heavily used in one area and infrequently used in another Inform EPM Report rationalization roadmap

future. Drivers in the predictive models include sales, shipments, advertising, consumer trends, pricing, product mix, and so on. The models take into account regional differences and in some cases go down to the product line and store levels. Where P&G has taken it to a whole new level is the way they present and interact with the models—they have developed "Business Spheres"—a self-contained meeting room wired with video conferencing and digital displays that surround managers and executives in the sphere. Remote participants see the same data on their iPads. They have over 40 interconnected Business Spheres around the world to facilitate interactive, real-time EPM visualization experiences.

Data Visualization

According to Ben Shneiderman, co-author of *Readings in Information Visualization: Using Vision to Think*, visual artifacts aid thought; in fact, they are completely entwined with cognitive action. With the advances in high-quality graphic data representation software, and the foundational work done by Edward Tufte, Stephen Few, and others, data visualization and infographics are becoming some of the most accessible methods of communicating and consuming data. The emergence of information visualization as a performance management tool is becoming pervasive and is attracting more business managers, students, and leaders to the field of analytics. Ideally, this new standard will extend to all areas of the management operating system to create the discipline of "visual performance management" including:

- Interactive reporting and analytics visualization, like what you've seen earlier in this chapter in the Patterns and New Insights section
- Visual modeling, predictive, and sensitivity analysis
- Visual planning and forecasting
- Visual strategy

Edward Tufte articulates the visual communication of information best. He said, "What is to be sought is the clear portrayal of complexity. Not the complication of the simple." Graphical displays should help the business user to think about what the data means. Some of his rules include a focus on information density (many data points in a small space), making large data sets accessible, encouraging comparison of dimensions and variables, and providing different levels of detail (fine-grained to summarized). He said "Above all else, show the data." And, as exemplified by the waterfall chart in Figure 4.12, visualization helps your data tell a story.

Another way to visualize data and tell a story is to embed one literally inside the other. For example, Figure 4.14 uses sparklines to emphasize the adjectives (increase, fell) describing the data. This way you can see just how much of an increase or how steep of a fall.

As expected, our revenue cycle follows its typical seasonality pattern this year with one unusual spike at the end of Q3 ⎓⌇⌇⌇ from our new channel marketing campaigns. Costs were in line with our operating margin goals and we met our monthly spend targets ⌇⌇⌇ in-line with the forecast. Forecast accuracy spikes near end of quarter as predicted ⌇⌇⌇ and the more we improve that the better uses we can make of discretionary spending.

Figure 4.14   Sparklines Embedded within Text

Enabling Technologies

EPM capabilities that are necessary to understand your data and information include:

- Financial and operational analytics
- Profitability analytics
- Predictive and statistical analytics
- Unstructured data inclusion
- Data consolidation and aggregation
- Data visualization

Components for Your EPM Roadmap

Not too dissimilar from the high-level architecture in Chapter 3 for reporting, the analytic components are designed in, at least, three layers as shown in Figure 4.15: the source data at the bottom, the data management and integration layer in the middle, and the end-user or analytic consumer at the top. The spider-web of connections from the front ends to the various analytic sources such as data marts and OLAP cubes is meant to convey the blending of subject matter in analytics. It's not uncommon to include customer, product, pricing, marketing, and supply-chain data in a single analysis.

Analytics is where OLAP engines shine. Their ability to pivot data across multiple dimensions (slice-and-dice) and start at the summarized level and drill into the details helps facilitate rapid analysis and faster time-to-insight.

An optional component in this architecture, which is just starting to gain attention and momentum in organizations, is an in-memory analytic appliance, for example Exalytics from Oracle or Hana from SAP, or smaller players like Altibase, Terracotta, and VoltDB. These appliances—which consist of bundled hardware and software—promise 10–100x faster performance of reporting and analytics, and are not inexpensive.

Potential Quick Wins

Any analytic initiative should be undertaken to better understand your business and to look for new insights to improve your results. This generally requires a solid grasp of your business model, value drivers, economic indicators, constraints and assumptions. Some business intelligence (BI) and analytic

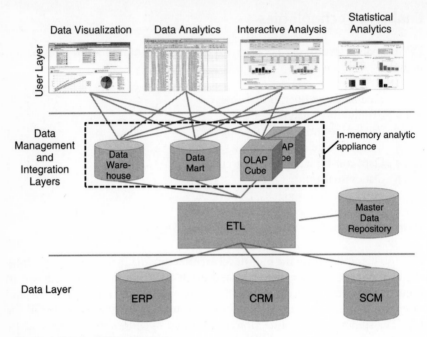

Figure 4.15   Analytics Architecture

vendors supply prebuilt applications that take data from a variety of standard source systems and present them ready to go "out of the box" with a minimum of tailoring or customization. And there are some universal analyses that should be easier to do than others. Some quick-wins could include:

Trending
- Historical actuals (sales, revenue, backlog, cost of goods sold [COGS], selling, general, and administrative [SG&A] expense, labor costs)
- Historical variance
- Intraquarter variance (when does your forecast go beyond 90% accuracy?)

Ratios
- Revenue per head (also known as productivity)
- Costs per head

Ranking
- Top/bottom customers (by volume, by sales)
- Top/bottom products (by volume, by sales)

One approach to adopting a culture of understanding and "competing on analytics," is to get some of these quick-wins so people can begin discussing the insights and asking more detailed questions—which will spawn a new series of investigations, analysis, and understanding.

Summary

In one study, the effective use of data and analytics correlated with a 5–6% improvement in productivity, and improved profitability.[3]

Many organizations have collapsed Gather and Understand into simple interactive reporting. This may work for some organizations, but with today's complexity, it is better to "un-collapse" these processes and provide enabling technologies to both areas—interconnected, of course. In this way, more powerful analytic capabilities can be brought to bear on the information you have gathered, new patterns can be spotted, and new hypotheses can be tested to find better ways to improve your financial and operational effectiveness. EPM is where we debate those hypotheses, simulate those tests, and come up with better ways of managing the business.

Notes

1. José Benki, et al., "Effects of Speech Rate, Pitch, and Pausing on Survey Participation Decisions," University of Michigan Institute for Social Research, May 2011.
2. Erik Brynjolfsson and Andrew McAfee, "Big Data: The Management Revolution," *Harvard Business Review*, October 2012.
3. Erik Brynjolfsson, Lorin M. Hitt, and Heekyung Hellen Kim, "Strength in Numbers: How Does Data-Driven Decision-Making Affect Firm Performance?" Social Science Research Network (SSRN), April 2011.

CHAPTER 5

Debate: Turning "What If" into "What's Next"

It is a capital mistake to theorize before one has data. Insensibly one begins to twist facts to suit theories, instead of theories to suit facts.

—SHERLOCK HOLMES

The promise of EPM is to provide a closed-loop framework for decision making, resource deployment, fewer surprises, and new insights. Most organizations are content with having EPM be about planning, reporting, and analytics, which theoretically gives you what you need. But there is a missing component, the most underused, underconnected, underappreciated part of the cycle: a system and process for facilitating, recording, communicating, and leveraging a robust debate about what's possible in the organization.

Looking into the Debate process in more detail, as shown in Figure 5.1, we see:

- **Goals.** The debate starts with the company goals and strategic objectives.
- **Optimize.** A robust debate can help vet the goals and objectives and make them more appropriate.
- **Financial and Operational Models.** What-if modeling should come out of isolated spreadsheets and exposed and collaborated on by people in all functions and layers of the business.
- **Facts.** Models are fed by historical trends, external facts, and other data that reflects actual performance.
- **Scenarios.** Multiple scenarios are generated and, in turn, vetted through additional analysis.

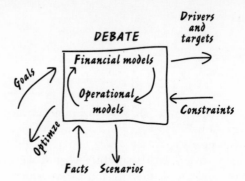

Figure 5.1   Close-Up of the Debate Process,
and Its Inputs and Outputs

- **Drivers and Targets.** Robust, shared, fact-based models and debates can uncover and prioritize the value drivers in the organization and the doable targets for each.
- **Constraints.** New constraints learned from the bottom up can be reused in financial and operational models to make them more accurate.

Imagine your strategic objectives from on-high come with a set of annual targets: "double-digit growth," "operation efficiencies of $1 billion," "improve net operating margins by 5%," "reduce headcount by 2,000." How did the powers-that-be derive those targets? Sometimes a rigorous study was commissioned from a highly regarded consulting firm that did a detailed time-and-motion and benchmark study, or perhaps some of your competitive peers just accomplished similar results, or it just "felt right" to the strategic planning committee. Sometimes it's just about survival. But how do you know it's the right thing to do? How can you improve confidence that it's even possible? How do you know it's not even a stretch and that even more is possible? And how do you ensure that changes in one target won't adversely affect other targets?

This next section of the EPM cycle allows you to prototype your business. It's where you model as many of the moving parts as practical and systematically look at a variety of what-if scenarios to finally come to a strategic plan that:

- Is doable
- Is based on the facts
- Takes into account past performance (which is no guarantee of future results!)

- Knows about your industry and seasonality
- Exploits known causes and effects
- Uses input and the expertise of a broad cross-section of your organization
- Is translatable into an actionable plan for the month, quarter, and year

Usually, business modeling, scenario planning, or long-range strategic planning are relegated to a select few analysts and advisors in Finance who use it to help inform the annual plan, targets, and company direction-setting. And there's nothing wrong with that. But what if we involved all areas of the organization, fed more internal and external data into the model, used sophisticated statistical techniques, and encoded our business model into scenarios? And what if we could quickly run hundreds of scenarios with a wide variety of variables where in the past we only had time and resources to run four or five simpler models? What if our models got smarter over time?

That's why I call it Debate: It engages more people throughout the organization to help aim the business in the right direction. It lets us work out the business model to help turn it into a plan that everyone can get behind. We create a system and process for debating what's possible.

People

As mentioned in Chapter 1, "If only people in our company knew what everyone in our company knows!" Too many times corporate analysts and planners have worked in a vacuum relying on macro-level reports and data to build their models, when down the hall or in the next building resides field staff with first-hand knowledge of what's really going on. For example, an analyst firm might predict that IT spending will be even for the remainder of the year, but your salespeople are talking to customer IT managers who are saying they are realigning their budgets to focus on products and services your company sells. This is certainly information that can cause your sales targets to go in two different directions: flat or up. That, in turn, will impact your sales headcount plan and variable compensation pool.

Many of your employees have details about customers, competitors, product issues, and so on that are not being captured, quantified, and used as a competitive advantage. In the past, it has been difficult to capture and codify this kind of information, but, as discussed in Chapter 4 in the Big Data and Predictive Analytics section, with new tools around unstructured data capture, semantic analysis, and technologies like "map reduce" (distributed, parallel processing), this kind of information is much easier to use in the Debate process. This now extends to information outside your four walls including news, financial information, social media, and so on.

Debate will produce relevant scenarios from which we choose the most likely one—and we turn that into our short-term action plan. It could also help inform how realistic our strategy is in the first place, and help us alter our strategy in the face of facts and fact-based predictions. In the Debate process, we learn more about our business and what makes it tick. Ideally, we want to learn about:

- **Constraints.** What are the lower limits of gross margin we need in order to run the business and return value to stakeholders? What's the ramp time for a new quota-carrying sales rep?
- **Assumptions.** Where do we think fuel prices will go this year, next year, and in five years? What do we think the cost of capital will be?
- **Drivers.** Do we know what those top drivers are that impact so many other metrics and outcomes in our organization? Have we prioritized them by materiality and volatility?
- **Targets.** Do we have baseline targets for financial and nonfinancial outcomes? Do we have stretch goals and worst-case targets?
- **Patterns.** Repeating results that can be correlated to time (like seasonality), external drivers (like a drop in sales volume as commodity prices increase), internal drivers (on-time-delivery fluctuations with changes in inventory levels and working capital). See Chapter 4 for additional patterns.
- **Risk tolerance.** Have we identified the risk components of our scenarios and quantified how they could impact results?

I once worked with a client in the energy sector who had multiple operations around the globe. Their annual production targets were centrally planned and decided at the corporate level. In a quarter with lean yields, Corporate decided to accelerate access to reserves, causing reserves to be depleted more rapidly than normal. They met their production targets that quarter and the next, but in the following year, their reserves were not at the levels expected by the board. When Corporate accused the regions of mismanaging resources, the regions reminded Corporate of the decisions made in the prior year, and the follow-on effects. The way the regional operations executives described it was that "Corporate has no memory." Had Corporate built a scenario model called "accelerate access to reserves," it could have helped in several ways:

- Documenting the decision
- Documenting the assumptions
- Calling out the constraints

- Showing the follow-on effects
- Showing the drivers that impact the outcomes
- Communicating expectations

The Process

So how does this work?

We need to look at four areas: the people, the process, the technology, and the data. These areas should work in concert to drive toward a common goal: developing the most realistic, probable model that helps you optimize your resources and deliver on your strategic goals. In addition, you would have a variety of models for different economic and competitive scenarios ready at hand for when market conditions change.

For example, you could have a scenario that models a doubling of fuel prices. It could predict a corresponding decrease in gross margin and a requirement for price adjustments. It would model out new prices by product given minimum margin targets for a period of time. Then, if fuel prices actually did double, that scenario could be activated to push out a revised quarterly sales plan using the new prices.

The model-building process usually starts with a brainstorming session, armed with observations, insights, and information from the Gather and Understand processes, to come up with possible alternatives and drivers of a scenario. The scenario is based on, or supports, a strategic imperative or objective that the company is having difficulty achieving or has concerns seeing a path to its execution. One structure that we can use to record the alternative scenarios is:

- Business Question/Outcome
  - Alternative 1: Name
    - Drivers with targets or changes in direction
  - Alternative 2: Name
    - Drivers with targets or changes in direction

For an example, let's take "profitable revenue growth" as the strategic imperative and begin to brainstorm the alternative scenarios and drivers that could emerge:

1. Question: How will we achieve our growth targets?/Outcome = 10% year-over-year (YOY) revenue growth
   a. Alternative: Organically
      i. Increase volume
      ii. Alter prices

      iii. New products

      iv. New services

      v. Bundling

      vi. Hire additional sales staff

      vii. Hire additional support staff

      viii. Increase number of leads

      ix. Improve lead conversion ratio

  b. Alternative: Through Acquisition

      i. Competitors

      ii. Adjacencies

  c. Alternative: Through Channel Partners

      i. Co-branding

      ii. Co-marketing

  d. Alternative: Through a blend of the previous three alternatives

2. Question: How will we achieve our margin targets/Outcome = 25% net margin

  a. Alternative: Reduce Direct Costs

      i. Outsource

      ii. Reduce inventories

  b. Alternative: Reduce Indirect Costs/Overheads

      i. Shared services

  c. Alternative: Increase Prices

  d. Alternative: Change our product mix (with more of a focus on highly profitable products)

  e. Alternative: Blend of alternatives

3. Question our assumptions

      i. Do we have the right strategy and targets?

      ii. Have we taken into account economic and market drivers?

      iii. What other events or impacts could happen, inside and outside of our control?

We can adopt any variety of alternative scenarios or blends of approaches in our models. Another example for revenue growth alternatives can be based on the business question "Build, borrow, or buy?"[1]:

1. How can we put our growth plans back on the right path? Outcome = 15% higher annual revenue from prior with a 5% improvement in operating margins and 2% improvement in gross margin.

  a. Alternative: Build

      i. People (number of full-time equivalents (FTE) by focus area by pay-grade)

      ii. Skills (percentage advanced degree, percentage certifications, number training hours per FTE)

   b. Alternative: Borrow

      i. Contracts (license fees, contingency coverage percentage, risk weighted)

      ii. Alliances (percent ownership in joint venture, number of points of contact)

   c. Alternative: Buy

      i. Ramp-Up (time to integration)

      ii. Talent (percent desirable staff retention)

For each of the drivers, we would select appropriate metrics, in parentheses beside each driver in the example. Of course, in order to see the effect those drivers have on the outcomes, we'll need to identify the intermediate value drivers that impact the outcome. For example, in the Borrow alternative, under Contracts, we'll need to know the average contract value and expected contract volume to get to a modeled revenue number.

Once we have identified the question, alternatives, drivers, and targets, we review all relevant facts available to us, including our analysis of:

- Prior results, trends, and seasonality
- Product, customer, and market profitability
- External/internal benchmarks
- Interconnections (Income Statement, Balance Sheet, Cash Flow)
- Balanced metrics (financial, operational/process, learning and growth/employee, customer)

Next, we use the predictive analytics at our disposal (see Chapter 4) to look at patterns and predicted paths based on variables and constraints. Finally, we iterate. Run the scenario, test the impact, measure the result, and recalibrate the model. This "test and check" method should not be discounted—a well-thought out set of assumptions and actions can yield new insights and cause-and-effect relationships that weren't known before.

So how do you select a scenario?

Scenarios

What-if scenarios are our attempts at making sense of what's happening, what can possibly happen, and of trying to minimize the impact of surprises. They're our way of being prepared for "eventualities" in business.

In A/B testing, you compare two possible scenarios, A and B. If A is better than B, go with A. By "is better" I mean achieves the target outcomes faster, more cost-effectively, and with appropriate risk. Then immediately do another A/B test. This is an example of continuous improvement: looking for appropriate alternatives, selecting one, implementing it, measuring the outcome and doing it over again. Sometimes a small incremental change can make a significant difference. Let's take some U.S. regional banks as an example. Based on publicly available data from 2010, let's look at RBS Citizens Bank compared to four other banks of similar size (average assets between $55 and $255 million):

- PNC Bank, NA
- Fifth Third Bank
- Suntrust Bank
- Comerica Bank

Using the techniques and tools from Chapter 4, we have done a benchmark analysis across seven KPIs (see Figure 5.2) and looked for areas of opportunity and their potential impact on value in the business.

In Figure 5.2, the closer a bubble is to the line at 0, the more opportunity there is to make a positive impact. And the size of the bubble tells us how much impact can be made (value creation in $ million).

We can quickly see from the bubble chart that Citizens Bank is the benchmark for Non Interest Expense (lower is better) at 2.4%. However, there is much room for improvement, and potential value impact, in Non Interest Income (revenue derived primarily from fees) and Net Interest Income (revenue derived from interest less associated expenses).

As shown in the chart, if we brought Non Interest Income in line with the benchmark company (Fifth Third Bank at 2.3%), then we could create $981 million in value (a direct cash impact). And if we could bring Net Interest Income in line with PNC Bank (the benchmark), we could create an additional $1,064 million in value. That's almost $2 billion in value if we made enough improvements to do what Fifth Third and PNC do. However Citizens bank is in different markets than Fifth Third and PNC with different mixes of products and services, different strategies, with different people. Let's assume we cannot get to the benchmark. Rather, what if we could make even a small dent in Non Interest and Net Interest Income? How much value could we stand to gain?

Doing the math, improving both of those key performance indicators (KPIs) by just 1% each could yield $49.9 million in value.

And we know 1% is possible in the industry since the competition is already doing better in those areas.

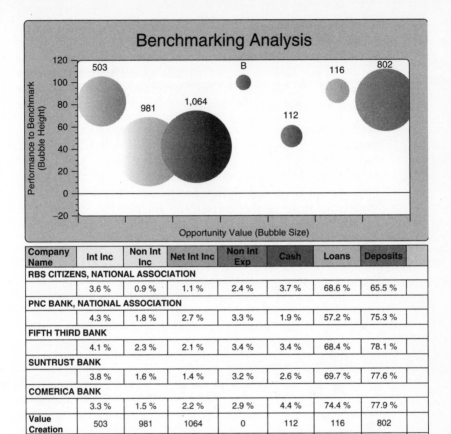

Company Name	Int Inc	Non Int Inc	Net Int Inc	Non Int Exp	Cash	Loans	Deposits	
RBS CITIZENS, NATIONAL ASSOCIATION								
	3.6 %	0.9 %	1.1 %	2.4 %	3.7 %	68.6 %	65.5 %	
PNC BANK, NATIONAL ASSOCIATION								
	4.3 %	1.8 %	2.7 %	3.3 %	1.9 %	57.2 %	75.3 %	
FIFTH THIRD BANK								
	4.1 %	2.3 %	2.1 %	3.4 %	3.4 %	68.4 %	78.1 %	
SUNTRUST BANK								
	3.8 %	1.6 %	1.4 %	3.2 %	2.6 %	69.7 %	77.6 %	
COMERICA BANK								
	3.3 %	1.5 %	2.2 %	2.9 %	4.4 %	74.4 %	77.9 %	
Value Creation	503	981	1064	0	112	116	802	
Cash Impact	503	981	1064	0	1902	1978	13671	

Figure 5.2   Benchmark Analysis for Citizens Bank, Q4 2010

So what do we need to do to improve Non Interest Income and Net Interest income by 1% each?

I'm sure there are a lot of banking operations and organizational change candidates to look at, but since this is a book about EPM, let's see how improving the management operating system of a bank can make at least a 1% positive difference in the business:

1. Better reporting (Chapter 3)
   - Alert branch management for accounts that perform below the average non interest income and target those accounts with high

assets under management for additional cross-selling activity. Track and report that activity.

- Provide a dashboard with net interest income by product (instrument) and give visibility to performance up and down the management chain.

2. Better analytics (Chapter 4)

- Perform customer profitability analysis and see potential better ways of segmenting customers (e.g., High Net Worth Individuals). Increase fees for customers with low balances, low account activity, or higher cost to serve.
- Perform root-cause analysis for underperforming investments.
- Model the effect of the lowest Non Interest Expense on Non Interest Income—perhaps being the benchmark on Expense is not the best thing for revenue growth!

3. Better modeling (Chapter 5—what we're doing right now)

- Perform additional pricing scenarios to see if fees are optimized (don't forget the value chain effect on other drivers, like customer attraction and retention).
- Perform inorganic growth scenarios using obvious M&A targets, look at the effect on both Net Interest and Non Interest Income.

4. Better planning (Chapter 6)

- Add some specific targets to the drivers of Non Interest Income, for example % cross-sell, and implement a sales program to incentivize better cross-selling behavior (don't forget to forecast and provide variance reporting).

Even with conservative costs of $10 million to implement some or all of those programs (consulting, software, training, and so on), that's not a bad return for a small investment and an incremental improvement.

Consider trying each of the initiatives as a test, one at a time. Then measure the impact the initiative has on the two KPIs. The challenge for A/B testing in this case is that it can be difficult to correlate the test with the results as causation. There are so many moving parts in the business and externally that are uncontrollable in an A/B test scenario—and without controlling the variables, you cannot prove that the initiative was the cause of the impact.

Resilience

As mentioned at the beginning of this chapter, having scenarios "ready at hand" to turn into an operational plan when circumstances dictate, is one of the key elements of Debate and one of the most underused parts of EPM. How do you determine what potential scenarios to create? For example, which of these scenarios would be most relevant for your organization:

- Warehouse costs double
- Cost of capital declines (more investment opportunities)
- Competition halves their prices
- Health care costs triple
- Heavy unwanted workforce attrition
- Demand declines for most profitable, most popular, stalwart, or flag-ship products
- You acquire your nearest competitor

Part of the debate process is to generate and select the most relevant scenarios to model and then either test or keep ready at hand for when a scenario becomes real. A great way to generate these is to ask not only your employees, management team, and the board of directors, but also your customers, suppliers, channel partners, industry analysts, competitors, and anyone who is involved in your ecosystem. Of course, to make any of these models meaningful, you'll need to know and quantify the underlying drivers.

Drivers: What Moves the Needle?

What drives value in your organization? You might say it's your people. Well, what drives the value of your people? It could be experience, skills, training, and certification. You might say your products drive value in your organization. What drives the value of your products? It could be quality, affordability, features and functionality, or uniqueness. Why do we need to quantify value? Because it shows us a path from our tactical, day-to-day activities and decisions, through our operational deployment of resources (people, time, capital, brand), to our overall strategic objectives and right down to the P&L statement, balance sheet, and cash flow.

Uncovering and knowing these drivers helps us not only in building models, but also in developing driver-based plans (Chapter 6), and in our enterprise reporting of metrics (Chapter 3). In Chapter 8, I go into more detail about metrics.

When we look at the constituent parts of each driver, or ask the question "what drives that," we get closer to possible root causes of improvements or performance hits—we go through a process of decomposing KPIs into their value drivers.

So let's take a look at drilling down through that value chain of drivers. In Figure 5.3 we decompose revenue and customer satisfaction.

We see some value-drivers, like brand in Figure 5.3, have multiple connection points, in this case, brand either drives, or is driven by, product quality, price, perceived value, pipeline conversion rate, and campaign effectiveness. With all these interconnections, and as one of the bridges between revenue and customer satisfaction, you would think brand is an important driver to measure, monitor, analyze, model, and plan for. Although metrics are discussed more in Chapter 8, it's worth noting here that one of the top brand metrics is "unaided awareness." An interesting analysis would be to

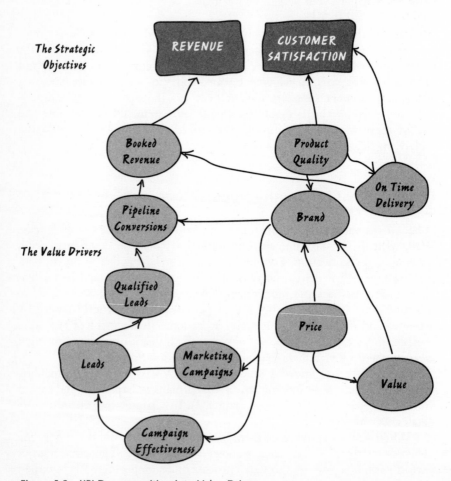

Figure 5.3   KPI Decomposition into Value Drivers

look for correlations between brand recognition, pricing, and sales pipeline conversion rates. And when a correlation is discovered, with rates, seasonality, limits, and so on, those facts can be added to a variety of models: your pricing model, lead generation models, sales models, marketing effectiveness models, and so on.

Uncovering root drivers is one of the keys to making useful models. In the sales commission model in Figure 5.4, the key drivers include quota, commission rate, and base salary. Some of the algorithms built into this model include estimated sales being based on prior achieved sales. Figure 5.4 is a sensitivity model, so each of those key drivers can be altered in a scenario to see the impact on outcomes. In this case the outcomes include estimated sales and compensation costs, number and percentage of reps making quota, and overall cost of sales. It also shows which reps will meet or exceed their on-target earnings (OTE).

When uncovering drivers for your models, consider using external, macro-economic indicators to help add the reality of market conditions. A quick example for the model in Figure 5.4 might be to add an algorithm to govern the estimated number of sales people—if the economy is growing, perhaps this number will grow proportionately or it could shrink if you expect sales people to leave when things start picking up—it might be a good idea to add employee satisfaction as a driver.

Debate Management

So far we have uncovered the drivers and selected scenarios in a model-building process and there's more to enabling and managing a debate than that. If we make good models, that's interesting but not very useful. If we make good models that keep getting better and help people throughout the business understand how plans, actions, and decisions support overall objectives, then we can help close the loop from strategy to sustainable execution and continuous improvement. Once we have our financial and operational models, here are six management operating steps to use them to manage the debate:

1. **Assign targets and time horizons.** Some targets are given (e.g., those from the board), some are unknown, and some are dependent on the outcome of the model. In multidimensional modeling tools, multiple targets can easily be assigned and managed (e.g., upside, downside, commit, stretch, etc.). Time horizons can be short term (next month), all the way to very long term (ten years), or, as some Japanese companies are purported to do—a hundred years.

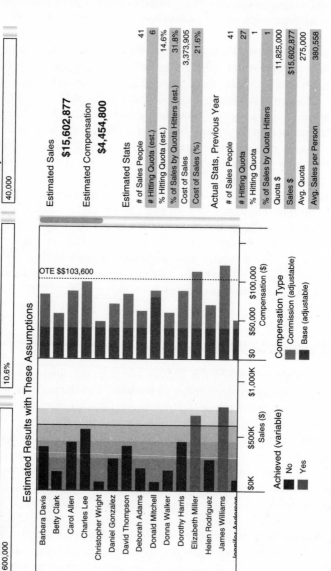

Figure 5.4 Model with Drivers and Assumptions
Courtesy Tableau Software Inc.

2. **Debate and vet the model itself, understand and record the assumptions, expose the algorithms, circulate it with subject matter experts, and "certify" it according to your governance methodology.** Risk weighting and risk profiles can also be included to add risk tolerance to the model.

3. **Run sensitivity analysis and perform predictive analysis (Chapter 4), creating versions with various targets for each model:**
   - Monte Carlo simulation may be an effective method for generating a possible range of targets or outcomes.
   - The number of versions depends on how strong or divergent various schools of thought are within your debate team. For example, one camp thinks SKU rationalization is the highest priority, one camp thinks price optimization is, so you do two models. The number of versions also depends on how many you can build how fast, for example using in-memory online analytical processing (OLAP) technology can technically do hundreds or thousands of complex multidimensional models quickly.

4. **Debate what the model says, especially about the outcomes.** Circulate the models to various functional groups (sales, marketing, operations, and so on), and involve multiple levels of the organization—from executives, through operational management, and on to front-line and back-office staff. To take this idea further, there is a methodology called predication markets that involves a wide variety of people voting (some have called it betting) on how close the results will be to the model or forecast. This is an interesting "crowd-source" method for collecting sentiments and I'll leave it up to you to explore that idea further.

   At this point, it may be useful to validate that the original strategic objectives and targets are actually possible to achieve. The debate process should help validate strategy and where there are material disconnects, the strategy itself could be revised.

5. **Agree on the "best" model.** That is, the one that seems most doable and most probable. Select it and turn it into a plan (more on this in Chapter 6). Remember that perfect is the enemy of good enough, so don't wait until your models are perfect to test them.

6. **When the plan goes out you get feedback, vet the feedback and put it back into the model.** This can take the form of new or more granular constraints communicated by the field, renegotiated or redistributed targets, additional assumptions, or more insights into drivers. Then start the process over again.

And, keep in mind that models are not real, but they are sometimes useful.

Enabling Technologies

There are a wide variety of modeling tools available today, ranging from prebuilt statistical models, through complete modeling and simulation environments that can be configured and tailored for your industry and your business. Some of the key components of most EPM-enabled organizations include:

- Financial modeling and scenario planning applications
- Statistical modeling packages
- Strategic Financial modeling (e.g., long-term P&L, balance sheet, and cash flow)
- Operational modeling (including activity-based management [ABM] models)
- Scorecards and strategy maps for high level outcome modeling
- OLAP engines and In Memory OLAP

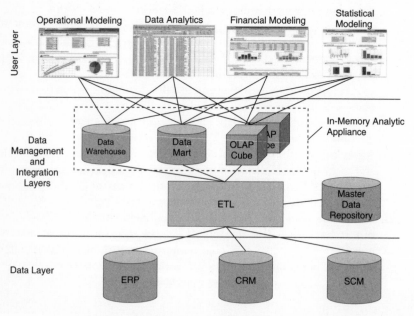

Figure 5.5   High-Level Architecture for Modeling

The key to managing and collaborating a wide variety of scenarios, each with their own versions, and each version having multiple dimensions, is OLAP technology. It also happens to be a popular technology for budgeting, planning, and forecasting—so when the model is ready to move into a plan of record, it can easily translate dimensions.

As shown in Figure 5.5, just like the other areas of EPM, the end user modeling tools rely on the same data management layer and tools which, in turn, get their data from source systems.

One big difference here, though, would be the presence of an OLAP history cube in order to use prior data to help predict trends, seasonality, growth rates, and so on.

Potential Quick Wins

The time it takes to build a model and run through the six stages of Debate management can take weeks or months and is an ongoing process. To get

Table 5.1 Examples of Models that Support Strategic Objectives

Strategic Objective	Models to Support the Debate
Profitable revenue growth	Sales comp model Pricing and discount models Cross-sell model Pipeline conversion model
Operational efficiency	Selling, general, and administrative (SG&A) ratio model Productivity models Raw material purchase models Shared-services models
Improved asset utilization	Preventative maintenance cycle models Asset lifetime models Production shift/hours models Occupancy rate models
Improve cash cycle velocity	Inventory models Receivables aging models Credit risk models Contract term models
Customer satisfaction	Call center staffing models Loyalty program models Promotion models Warranty models
Employee engagement	Undesirable attrition models Employee training investment models Benefits models Compensation models

started with the management operating system way of debating the business, you can generate a simple model and pilot the six stages with a smaller group of stakeholders to show the benefits of exposing models and generating collaborative debate on drivers, targets, constraints, and assumptions. The possibilities of what to model are endless, and the best place to start is with strategic objectives. Table 5.1 shows a composite sample of some models clients have built in support of strategic objectives.

Summary

This is the one area of EPM that is the least exploited and possibly the best positioned for competitive advantage. Most companies do reams of reporting, a plethora of planning, and ample analytics, but when it comes to models and what-if scenarios, they are usually ad hoc, sparse, hidden on someone's C drive, or hidden on someone's wish list.

This part of the management cycle connects the past to the future. If all of the reporting and analytics we do helps us understand where we are and why we got what we got, this part of the cycle helps us sort out where we want to go, and what's possible.

Ideally, this area of EPM helps enable a robust debate in the business. Hopefully, there is already plenty of debating in your organization amongst teams: What's the right course of action, what's the best use of resources, how much, how fast, when, and where? Yet many of these debates consist of conjecture, opinion, agenda, and political positioning. What would it look like if your debate was a process with some rigor enabled by data and systems? Instead of operating in a vacuum, the entire business can be aligned on "what's possible" and "what's next."

Note

1. Will Mitchell and Laurence Capron, *Build, Borrow, or Buy: Solving the Growth Dilemma*, Harvard Business Press, 2012.

CHAPTER 6

Commit: Bringing Accountability and Focus to the Enterprise

> Unless commitment is made, there are only promises and hopes; but no plans.
>
> —PETER F. DRUCKER

In any organization, how do you know who is "on the hook" for delivering what results? You probably know what your objectives are, and those of your team, and you may know the overall corporate objectives and targets for the year or the quarter, but how much visibility do you have into who is responsible to deliver what, by when? In many organizations, this is recorded in budgets, plans, and forecasts.

The inputs and outputs of the Commit process (see Figure 6.1) include:

- **Drivers and Targets.** The real value drivers of the business are exposed in the Debate process and the "right" scenario for success, including validated targets, is used to create commitments.
- **Constraints.** The financial and operational planning processes uncover new constraints that will improve your models.
- **Financial and Operational Plans.** Interrelated, enterprise planning covering all areas of the business are created, shared, and used to help make decisions in all areas of the business.
- **Decide/Execute.** Commitments (who will do what, by when and where) guide decisions you make to execute your strategic objectives.
- **Reforecast.** Based on actual results, you may need to adjust your forecasts and plans up or down. The faster and more accurately you can respond to events will give you a competitive advantage.

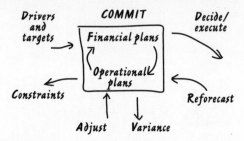

Figure 6.1   Close-Up of the Commit Process, and Its Inputs and Outputs

- **Adjust.** What you learn from gathering and understanding results may prompt you to adjust your plans.
- **Variance.** How you track to budget, plan, and forecast, will cause different actions in all business functions in the organization.

In general, the process works like this: The company has decided what its high-level targets for the year and quarter are for revenue, expenses, capital expenditures, headcount, and so on. Hopefully it has vetted these targets during a robust, fact-based debate using historical information, external data, market research, statistics, scenarios, and so on as described in Chapter 5. Then the targets are parceled out to individual business functions, regions, and teams to divide the targets into accountable groups. This is called "top-down" planning. Sometimes it stops there—the edict from on high—"you will deliver these numbers . . . period." In more enlightened organizations, there is a give-and-take process in three directions: top-down, bottom-up, and side-to-side (see Figure 6.2). Once the targets are parceled out by region and by quarter, those responsible for that region may further parcel out that subtarget to their teams (sales managers for example) and ask them to consider how doable that target is given their particular teams, market conditions, customer base, and so on. If there's an issue in one region, a manager can assign a higher proportion of burden to a region that can absorb it. Side-to-side managers consult with their counterparts in other areas of the business to tweak their forecasts. For example, a sales manager in a region where product X is very popular would consult with the product marketing manager for product X to get more insight on upcoming features and release schedules, and might also consult with delivery operations to see if there are any production or inventory constraints to expect next quarter or even next year.

Those teams closest to the customer or the market have some valuable knowledge that is usually locked away in their private spreadsheets that, if unlocked, can help the company get smarter at planning and competing.

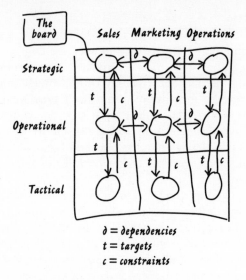

Figure 6.2   Top-Down, Bottom-Up, and
Side-to-Side Iterative Planning

If they believe that the target is unreasonable or not achievable, they can communicate exactly why back up the chain to the top where the corporate targets can be rebalanced across different teams or different time periods. It's those reasons why that provides valuable information that can be reused to make the financial and operational models better so that the next time you run the Debate–Commit cycle, it's more accurate or probable. Some of the bottom-up information to capture that helps make your plans and models better includes:

- New competition in a region can put new price pressures on deals.
- Open headcount on sales reps can be taking much longer to fill, delaying time to sales.
- New products, which may form a large part of the top-down plan, may not be resonating with a particular market or customer type.
- Customers may be moving out of a territory.
- Economic issues may be causing deals to take much longer to close.
- Material costs or availability could be impacted adversely by weather or economic conditions.

The goal is to capture those constraints and assumptions and learn from them and continually improve the planning and modeling cycle.

Accountability

The number (and type) of clients that do not have targets for each of their financial and operational objectives is surprising. Some will say they want to improve operating margins but won't say by how much. Some will say they want profitable revenue growth but won't specify how much profit or what rate of revenue growth. Or if they do, it's just a top-line number. "5% revenue growth and 5% improvement in operating margin" is great, but is that just across the board or a blended number based on faster revenue growth from some products in some regions to make up for flat or no growth from other products or regions?

The goal of planning is to provide an appropriate level of accountability throughout the organization while remaining nimble enough to make resource deployment changes to react to changes in the market. Coming back to our multidimensional concepts from Chapter 2, a plan must include all of the right dimensions of the business, but not too many. It must include the right level of detail: not too much, not too little—although most clients I've seen could stand to do with less granular planning. The most common standard dimensions to plan to include:

- Time (an annual plan broken up into months/quarters is usually sufficient for revenue and expense)
- Accounts (sales, operating expenses, headcount, and so on)
- Business units/geography (down to regions or territories)

After those top three, it depends on a few things. It depends on what you are planning and it depends on how your business works. You might also organize your plan by:

- Product line (perhaps down to product, hopefully not down to SKU level)
- Customer type (large, medium, small enterprise; public sector, but hopefully not down to named customer)
- Channel (direct sales force, partner sales, on-line, values at risk [VARs], etc.)

There is a trade-off between the number of dimensions and level of detail you plan for and the value they give the organization. If you get to too low a level of detail, or you have too many dimensions, people will spend an inordinate amount of time on the planning process with little corresponding benefit.

Annual Sales Plan
Rep: Marlene Reid

Account	Q1	Q2	Q3	Q4	FY13 Total
Quota	600,000	400,000	400,000	600,000	2,000,000
Travel and Entertainment expense	12,000	6,000	8,000	12,000	38,000

Figure 6.3   A Simple Plan

For example, here's a sales plan for a single sales rep in a software company. The first view (Figure 6.3) is a high-level plan, and the second view (Figure 6.4) is at a more detailed level with more dimensions.

The high-level plan (Figure 6.3) is easy and fast to do, and shows the same level of overall accountability as the detailed plan (Figure 6.4). If you have 500 sales reps, this may be the right level of information to communicate up the chain, and let the reps individually manage how they get to their quarterly number.

The detailed plan, however, takes more time and thought by each rep to put together. It adds two levels of detail: monthly quota (instead of quarterly) and includes a product dimension. It may make sense to plan quota by product—reminding the rep that they are accountable for driving sales in multiple product areas. However, it may not make sense to plan travel and entertainment (T&E) expense by product area, as sales trips are usually made to a customer regarding multiple products. So we end up with sparse information around travel expenses.

The additional detail in the monthly spread lets us take into account historic seasonality patterns acknowledging that the plan isn't evenly spread within the quarter.

What do we get from all the extra details in the plan? It usually matters in at least two areas: resource planning and shortfalls. By knowing what the sales levels will be for each month, sales managers from other areas (e.g., presales support and marketing) can plan sales engineering, proposal writing, and field marketing events to coincide with the level of activity indicated by the quota plan. It also lets each product manager know roughly how much to produce each month.

Where there is a material shortfall to the plan, uncovered during a forecast perhaps, sales management will want to drill down into the details to find out the source of the shortfall. In the detailed example in Figure 6.4, you could drill down into a particular month or even at a product level.

Annual Sales Plan
Rep: Marlene Reid

Product	Account	Jan	Feb	Mar	Q1	Apr	May	Jun	Q2	Jul	Aug	Sep	Q3	Oct	Nov	Dec	Q4	FY13 Total
Core Software	Quota	60,000	120,000	100,000	280,000	30,000	90,000	60,000	180,000	30,000	90,000	60,000	180,000	60,000	120,000	100,000	280,000	920,000
	T&E expense	6,000	4,000	2,000	12,000	3,000	2,000	1,000	6,000	3,000	2,000	1,000	6,000	6,000	4,000	2,000	12,000	36,000
Ancillary Software	Quota	15,000	30,000	25,000	70,000	7,500	22,500	15,000	45,000	7,500	22,500	15,000	45,000	15,000	30,000	25,000	70,000	230,000
	T&E expense				—				—				—				—	
Implementation Services	Quota	30,000	58,000	50,000	138,000	15,000	58,000	30,000	103,000	15,000	58,000	30,000	103,000	30,000	58,000	50,000	138,000	482,000
	T&E expense				—				—				—				—	
Training Services	Quota	9,000	18,000	15,000	42,000	4,500	13,500	9,000	27,000	4,500	13,500	9,000	27,000	9,000	18,000	15,000	42,000	138,000
	T&E expense				—				—				—				—	
Maintenance Fees	Quota	15,000	30,000	25,000	70,000	7,500	22,500	15,000	45,000	7,500	22,500	15,000	45,000	15,000	30,000	25,000	70,000	230,000
	T&E expense				—				—				—				—	
Total Products	Quota	129,000	256,000	215,000	600,000	64,500	206,500	129,000	400,000	64,500	206,500	129,000	400,000	129,000	256,000	215,000	600,000	2,000,000
	T&E expense	6,000	4,000	2,000	12,000	3,000	2,000	1,000	6,000	4,000	2,000	2,000	8,000	6,000	4,000	2,000	12,000	38,000

Figure 6.4 A More Detailed Plan

Accountability, expressed in an organization's plan, should include the following three components:

1. What is being committed (dollar level, volume, percentage change)
2. By whom (business unit, country/region, territory/team, individual rep)
3. By when (monthly, quarterly)

Since planning and forecasting aren't exact, some leeway is given, especially on ranges of the plan or forecast. In EPM, these ranges are captured in versions of the plan. For each of the cells (i.e., intersection of product, account, and month for each rep) in Figure 6.4 there could be three plan versions, thus giving management some insight into a range of possible values so they can plan accordingly. Of course, it's more work to capture the plan at that level of detail; however, it may be worth it. Some common plan or forecast versions include:

1. Downside
2. Upside
3. Commit

Gaming the System

Did you know that all sales people are bilingual? They speak their native language and at least one other: salesese. You've probably heard some of it: sandbagging, long-shots, bird-dogs, low-ball, slam-dunk, spiff, seymore, smoke screen, spray-and-pray, stall, sleevies.[1] This lingo has evolved over the years to try and overcome just how difficult it can be to describe where you are in a sales cycle and where you think you're going. If you're going to make your number, as a company, a territory, or even an individual rep, you have to speak a common language in order to engage in a debate with the right people, at the right time, to determine the right actions to take to reach a specific target—and then you have to record that commitment in a shared, collaborative system that integrates the numbers, assumptions, and drivers.

These commitments not only show *how* you're going to achieve the results you agreed on, they also help you take corrective action. A rigorous, standard planning methodology helps reduce finger pointing and blame by showing direct cause and effect of variance. A shortfall could be due to a rep, a product line, and entire territory, higher discounting, lack of spend management, and so on. When the root cause is determined, that information can be fed back into the model that the plan was derived from, so the model is better for the next cycle. Also, when more people have visibility to variance to commitments, there is generally more accountability as an entire community (a sales team, a product marketing team, a customer service team) can see and share in the variance and help the team out to make up shortfalls. This is true not only for sales planning, but all of the planning you do in your organization.

Enterprise Planning and Forecasting

There are many kinds of plans in any organization. The kind of plan depends on what the plan is trying to accomplish, who the audience is, and how frequent and granular the plan needs to be. Here are the most common types of EPM plans:

Strategic Planning
- Annual budget
- Long-range plan/strat plan
- Cash-flow forecast
- Balance sheet plan

Finance Planning
- Annual operating plan (AOP)
- Revenue and expense plan
- Sales plan
- Capital expenditure plan

Operational Planning
- Workforce plan
- Project financial plan
- Marketing plans (including category plan, campaign plan, etc.)
- Demand plan

Forecasts
- Sales forecast
- Expense forecast
- Demand forecast
- Project forecast

Many of these plans are interrelated and components from one can and should feed another as shown in Figure 6.5. For example, the total planned salary and benefits expenses from the workforce plan can feed the AOP and the expense plan—at different levels of detail if required, by team, by geography, or by individual if required.

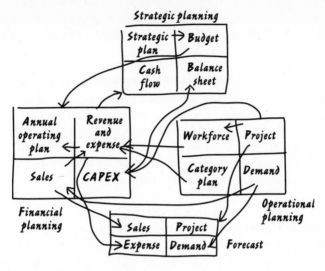

Figure 6.5   Integrated Plan Types

Integrated sales and operational planning (S&OP), developed by Oliver Wight in the 1980s is another type of plan that connects manufacturing output with expected sales levels and can be enabled by EPM.

Driver-Based Planning

All plans can be considered driver-based if you single out volume and rate as drivers. But modern day driver-based planning is more than that. It's about uncovering the key drivers that "move the needle" of the top line and bottom line. What drives volume? And what drives rates? The same processes used to decompose metrics in Chapter 5 (in the Drivers: What Moves the Needle? section) and also shown in Chapter 8 (in the Functional Value Maps section) is used to uncover those key drivers used in a driver-based plan. Drivers take out some of the gaming from plans and forecasts since the plan is based on historical rates, known patterns (like seasonality), and forward-looking assumptions for each key plan driver. For example, a sales plan for next quarter based on key drivers could have each rep enter the following information:

- Number of planned face-to-face meetings: 24
- Number of planned demos: 10

Knowing that in the past the average sale conversion happens after three face-to-face meetings and two demos, the rep would be expected to close five sales (10 demos/2 demos per sale). An average selling price in that region of $5,000 gives a quarterly forecast for that rep of $25,000. This leads to a few interesting ideas:

- The rep will work towards fulfilling the behavior that drives the outcome—they will work to book 24 meetings and 10 demos.
- Constraints are exposed—in this case, demos are limiting the possible number of sales since, on average, a sale is made with three face-to-face meetings, the rep could have eight sales, but can't (or isn't) planning to do enough demos—six more would be needed. Is the constraint presales resources? Time in the demo lab?

In the real world, management still has the prerogative to override a driver-based plan. They may have insights that may not be quantifiable about a particular rep or region and want to temper the plan accordingly. However, it would be worth a look to see if any of that information can be quantified. For example, the sales manager knows the rep is capable of a higher plan than $25,000 for the quarter and would override it to $30,000. Yet looking at the historical data for that rep it's noticed that she consistently achieves 10% above plan, so why not let the planning system override the inputted plan to $27,500?

Forecast Accuracy

Organizations have always had a concern with forecast accuracy, but it's being felt more keenly now.

So how does EPM help address forecast accuracy concerns? Here are nine areas to look at:

1. Have a formal forecast process in place—companies are trending towards rolling sales and expense forecasts.
2. Use a multidimensional tool so that forecasts can roll up by geo, product, customer type, and so on as the business demands. Multi-dimensional tools also let you add weighting, bias, and probabilities (multidimensional databases are discussed in Chapter 4).
3. Improve the quality of the data—if forecasts are based on prior period actuals, make sure the basis of your forecast is reliable.
4. Measure and report forecast errors—expose the causes of the problem, and take action to fix them. Use data mining tools to locate sources and trends of errors.
5. Senior management must make a commitment to improving forecast accuracy. Their variable compensation should be tied to it.

6. Communicate the impact of poor forecast accuracy to everyone in the organization who has anything to do with forecasting, including opportunities lost with mismanaged discretionary spending as well as the impact on stock price caused by a wide miss or revised earnings estimates to the market.

7. Make assumptions follow the forecast. In other words, fully expose the assumptions that make up the forecast by quantifying the assumptions or, at a minimum, including narratives with each forecast—to the most granular level manageable (many forecasting tools now let you do cell-level annotation, for example).

8. Look at new methodologies such as risk-weighting, predictive models and prediction markets.[2]

9. Continuously learn about best practices in forecasting.[3]

Rolling Forecasts

Many organizations are doing away with the annual budget and replacing it with a continuous planning and forecasting process. With a rolling forecast the number of periods forecasted remains constant. For example, if you do a five-quarter rolling forecast at the end of the current quarter, a new forecast is added for five quarters out. So you are always forecasting for five quarters. In this way, we're not waiting for Q4 before we have a plan or forecast for next year.

Resource Optimization

All of this shared, coordinated, and integrated planning is useful only if it helps us make better decisions on where to focus our attention and where to spend our time and money. This is true for:

- When, where, and how much to deploy our people
- When and where to focus our marketing efforts, and at what level of investment
- Where to invest capital, hedge, and leverage debt
- What products to focus on and which ones to retire
- Which clients to pay more attention to

Let's illustrate how enterprise planning helps us optimize resource decisions with another sales example. Perhaps your sales forecast is behind your revenue plan by a wide margin. You investigate the pipeline and look for the largest deals, furthest along in the sales cycle, with the highest probability of closing. You would then focus your presales or technical resources on spending additional time with those clients helping them see the value of your wares through better demos or proofs of concepts. Simultaneously, you refocus your marketing efforts and marketing spend on those products being considered by that narrowed list of top prospects to help provide air cover and support to the sales team. You also revise the demand plan accordingly so production is able to supply new concentrations of specific products given the new mix expected by the end of the quarter.

Having an integrated planning and forecasting process and system that cover financial, operational, and strategic drivers lets you react faster and more effectively to constantly changing business circumstances.

Enabling Technologies

Since EPM planning systems generate their own data, the budget, plan, and forecast data, they need their own repository. This is usually stored in a combined multidimensional (online analytical processing [OLAP]) and relational store specifically for plans. You don't want to store your plan data back in your transactional systems since they are stored at different levels of detail, at different times, and with multiple versions.

Ingredients for Your EPM Roadmap

Figure 6.6 shows the common components of an enterprise planning system and their relation to transactional and "actuals" data repositories. Just like other EPM components, planning systems use different front ends to match the audience and purpose of the plan. More applications now are including mobile components that let field representatives update forecasts in real time from the field on their tablets and smart phones.

Potential Quick Wins

While you're refreshing your EPM roadmap (see Chapter 9), you can at least replace all those spreadsheets and all that manual consolidation and tracking with an automated cloud planning system. Think of this as a prototype for an enterprise-level integrated planning system. The setup is quick and it gets your planning contributors and forecasters to start thinking about the process, about multidimensionality, and about real-time consolidation.

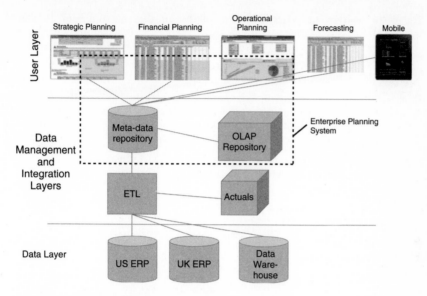

Figure 6.6   High-Level Planning Architecture

For example, a cloud-based sales compensation planning system took two days to prototype, another two days to refine the allocation and spread logic behind the scenes, and a week to deploy and train users on how to enter their plans on the Web (and from mobile devices). The forecast is always consolidated so that sales management can see in real time how the forecast is shaping up. One of the newest cloud platforms that does this is Anaplan.

Summary

As former U.S. President Dwight D. Eisenhower said, "Plans are worthless. Planning is essential." I might disagree that plans are worthless, so long as we remember they are inaccurate predictions used to document our debate about what we want to happen. Of course the process of planning is invaluable—it helps you question assumptions, understand constraints, prioritize resources, and shape decisions. Enterprise planning has been called the cornerstone of EPM, and it's usually the first initiative that EPM organizations undertake. EPM done right means that your plans are based on a model built in a debate that was fed by facts about the business, and it shares common business rules, formulae, and master data with the phases of the management operating system.

Notes

1. I recently heard the term "sleevies" from a sales manager who uses it to describe those opportunities that reps keep "up their sleeves" and not in the pipeline.
2. Christoph Hueglin and Francesco Vannotti, http://portal.acm.org/citation.cfm?id=502512 .502578 and Renée Dye, www.mckinseyquarterly.com/Strategy/Strategy_in_Practice/The_ promise_of_prediction_markets_2114_abstract
3. E.g., see the International Institute of Forecasters, http://forecasters.org

CHAPTER 7

Execute: From Insight to Actions to Results

Vision without execution is hallucination.

—THOMAS A. EDISON

Let's take a look at the management operating system in action. You can break down the "E" in EPM to any part of the enterprise: sales, marketing, order to cash, supply chain, workforce, and so on. You can even follow the chain to organizations you partner with. When you focus on each of these parts, they follow the same closed-loop cycle, work off the same data, metadata, and rules, and are enabled by the same technology. The more you unify these components for each part of the enterprise, the less you spend on reinventing the wheel, reworking reports, plans, models, and analyses, and the more you can agree on the numbers.

Everything Is Connected

In Chapter 2, in the Macro and Micro section, I mentioned how the cycle can exist at many levels of the organization. The cycle works at the corporate level, the business-unit level, the business-function level, and the team level. And each level can be interrelated. For example, in Figure 7.1, the commitments at the corporate level can feed the debate at the business-unit level, or can just become the commitment at the business-unit level, and what the business-unit level gathers and understands can feed into the corporate gathering process.

To extend that thinking beyond the four walls of your organization, into your value ecosystem, as shown in Figure 7.2, the cycle can extend to your suppliers, customers, and other partners.

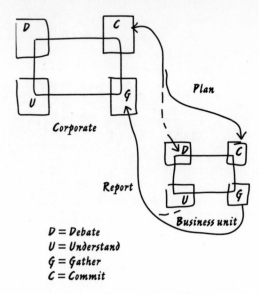

D = Debate
U = Understand
G = Gather
C = Commit

Figure 7.1   The Management Operating
System Works from Corporate to Business-Unit
Levels

In advanced uses of EPM, organizations invite entities beyond their control to participate—to consume and contribute information—in the management operating system. Some examples include:

- Letting customers enter expected demand levels for future time periods, which feeds into your demand forecast

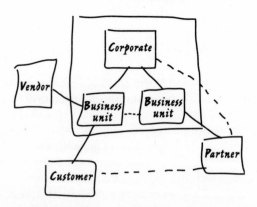

Figure 7.2   EPM Outside of the Four Walls of
Your Organization

- Letting suppliers see a summarized, sanitized (anonymous) version of your demand forecast or pipeline to know how to stock raw material levels to meet potential demands
- Letting staffing companies know about upcoming vacancies or over-time requirements to help staff to expected levels of work

Sales Performance Management

In his easily accessible book *What the Customer Wants You to Know*, Dr. Ram Charan says that companies need to focus on the customer rather than their own product or service's features and benefits, and change the way they sell. You have to understand your clients' business and strategic objectives, he says, in order to work backward and see how your wares can positively impact those objectives. Most salespeople show how they will reduce their prospects' costs, and don't touch on improving revenues, margin, brand, market share, cash flow, and so on. So how would EPM work inside your organization to help manage the soon-to-be-transformed world of sales?

It's useful to keep in mind what the top sales-management priorities are (so that you can link sales analysis back to strategy). These top sales-management priorities can each be enhanced and enabled by EPM:

1. Optimize the pipeline—from generating leads to converting prospects to customers
2. Improve sales processes and team structures
3. Align sales and marketing more closely
4. Improve pricing effectiveness
5. Analyze customer buying patterns
6. Automate sales operations
7. Improve channel effectiveness
8. Add customer relationship management (CRM) analytics on top of your CRM system
9. Enhance sales team focus and alignment
10. Revise compensation and commission programs[1]

So, from that list, you can see a sales performance management (SPM) dashboard having the following tabs:

- Marketing (including lead generation)
- Customer (including sales stages)
- Channel (including pipeline)
- Team (including compensation)

Taking it a step further, and making SPM more holistic (part of EPM), you could also include tabs for:

- Development (visibility into the product pipeline, and launch dates)
- Support (a look at the most common customer issues, customer satisfaction, etc.)
- Finance (how each sales rep/team contributes to revenue, margin, cash flow, days sales outstanding)
- Operations (time to delivery, etc.)

And based on Dr. Charan's comments, if I were a sales manager, I would want to keep my eye on some of these operational sales metrics:

- Time spent on prospect research and peer benchmarking
- Number of features directly matched with prospect objectives
- Rank of importance of key business indicators (revenue growth, margin, cash cycle, etc.)
- Cash and recurring benefit available to prospect company with 1%, 5%, 10% improvement on two or more financial measures using the proposed solution (see the Scenarios section of Chapter 5).

Sales Operations Performance

How do you measure and plan for the success of sales operations? While some companies use sales ops as the reporting and analysis arm of sales, others are transforming sales ops to be a strategic partner in the sales, marketing, and customer satisfaction functions: bridging activities and results across those three areas of the business. So how do you measure success for a smart sales operations team?

Let's divide sales operations performance drivers (these could be metrics, key performance indicators [KPIs], measures, or processes—any of which is a key driver of value in sales operations) into three categories: strategic (at the top level of the organization), operational (where planning and resource allocation live), and execution (the tactical layer of the business). Here are some of the more popular drivers:

Strategic
- Sales revenue
- Forecast accuracy
- Territory design effectiveness
- Quota

- Productivity
- Compensation
- Average selling price (ASP)
- Time to revenue
- Open headcount
- Pipeline
- Product and channel mix
- Customer acquisition efficiency
- Demand planning
- Channel efficiency
- Selling, general, and administrative (SG&A) expense
- Net operating profit

Operational

- Product training hours
- Contract quality
- Request for Quote/Proposal quality
- Order management
- Product certification
- Collateral effectiveness
- Commission management
- Sales entity reviews
- Sales training hours
- Methodology usage
- Reference quality
- Competitive intelligence
- Sales certification
- Sales meeting effectiveness
- Award programs
- Sales behavior

Execution

- Sales force automation system usage
- Expense management
- Territory management
- Sales activities
- Customer relationship management system usage
- Channel conflict
- Dispute resolution
- Customer face time
- Quota accuracy
- Commission accuracy

- Sales initiatives
- Sales call prep
- Forecast accuracy
- Deal registration quality
- Sales incentive overspend
- Customer intelligence

For those drivers that are most material and most volatile—meaning they make the biggest difference and change frequently, so you want to keep an eye on them—you run them through the management operating system to look for your top sales operation performance management initiatives. More on this in Chapter 9.

Order to Cash Performance Management

As with any transactional process used to run the organization, EPM sits on top to help manage the process and the overall organization. Order to cash is no different. Improving the cycle time and amount of effort to get from an actual sale to cash in the bank can have a material impact on the business. Let's take a look at a standard order-to-cash transactional process in Figure 7.3.

This process is:

- Transactional
- Granular (detailed)
- Daily
- May have multiple versions (per different business units or countries)
- May store its data in a variety of systems (general ledger, CRM, credit system, contracts)

When you connect the management operating system on top of all of this transactional data, it might logically look like Figure 7.4

Figure 7.3   Standard Order to Cash Process

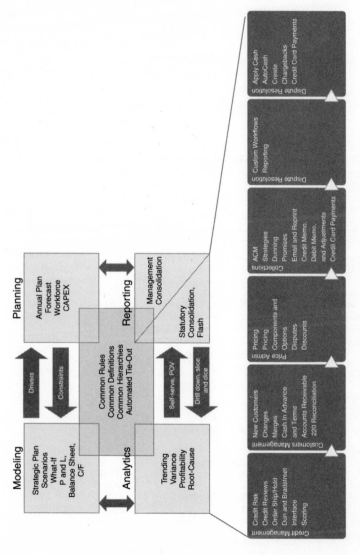

Figure 7.4   Management Operating System on Top of Order-to-Cash Transactions

Some common order-to-cash performance management initiatives could include:

- Credit risk analysis (including customer segmentation)
- Receivable analytics (aging, days sales outstanding [DSO], billing error rate, cycle times, cost per invoice)
- Backlog variance
- Bank reconciliation (automated reconciliation management)
- Cash conversion efficiency trends
- Cash-flow forecasting
- Pricing/discount analysis

For one client, their order-to-cash performance management roadmap included, along with broader EPM initiatives, initiatives aligned to the corporate priorities as shown in Table 7.1.

Table 7.1 EPM and Order-To-Cash Performance Management Initiatives

Corporate Priority	Enterprise Performance Management	Order-To-Cash Performance Management
Improve earnings before interest, taxes, depreciation, and amortization (EBITDA) margin	Selling, general and administrative (SGA) expense, and cost of goods sold (COGS) analysis Workforce planning	Credit risk analysis Customer profitability
Align pricing with value	Demand planning Price/mix modeling	Discount analysis Pricing analysis
Invest in the business	Strategic finance models Capital expenditure (CAPEX) planning	Customer/product profitability
Improve and manage demand	Demand planning Variance analysis	On-time delivery analysis Transportation cost analysis
New product development priority	Percentage of sales from new product analysis (and cross-sell analysis)	Invoice terms models Customer financing models
Manage debt	Balance sheet modeling, planning and forecasting	Cash-flow forecast
Improve working capital	Days payable outstanding (DPO) reporting and analysis	Days sales outstanding (DSO), Days in inventory (DII) reporting and analysis

Supply Chain Performance Management[2]

Managing the performance of your suppliers, a critical component of overall supply and demand chain management, can have a material impact on your company's revenue growth and operating margin. Not investing in how you manage supplier performance, especially in a down economy, can have a negative impact on your profits, assets, and cash flow.

Starting with the overall EPM framework, I have found that it works well to focus on supplier performance or any dimension of the supply chain. The goal of the framework is to help manage the process of strategy to execution. You already have overall company strategic objectives: a certain level of revenue growth at a particular target margin, or an expected level of market share and brand recognition, for instance. Within those corporate objectives, you have specific supplier performance objectives: a certain level of material quality, cycle times, inventory levels, and so on. The challenge is to ensure that you efficiently—and sustainably—execute on those objectives and continuously improve your fact-based decision-making capabilities that get you closer to realizing your strategy.

To do this, you must be able to rigorously answer these questions: "What do we want to happen with suppliers, and how do we want it to happen?" and "What actually happened, and why did it happen?" The supplier performance management operating system that helps answer these questions is shown in Figure 7.5.

The framework says that you take your strategic supplier objectives and you debate them. Are you able to achieve those objectives? Do you have sufficient capital, people, customers, and markets? What if you negotiated different terms with suppliers? What if you acquired some of your suppliers? What if you outsource more logistics services? What if fuel costs become even more unpredictable? Should you buy or build a certain component? This is where you build financial and operational models to record constraints and vet your assumptions about suppliers. Instead of a few spreadsheets run by a few analysts, this is an open process by the executive management team from all business functions—sales, marketing, procurement, and customer and supplier operations—with multiple scenarios recorded in a multidimensional system. It includes historical performance data as well as internal and external benchmarks to address questions such as "How do we do better than last time?" and "How do we do better than industry averages?" Once the most likely scenario is agreed upon (after a healthy and rigorous debate), this model forms the basis of your suppler plans.

Those plans form the basis for how you decide how and when you are going to deliver products and services to customers and consume materials and resources from suppliers. It's the commitment your managers, sales reps,

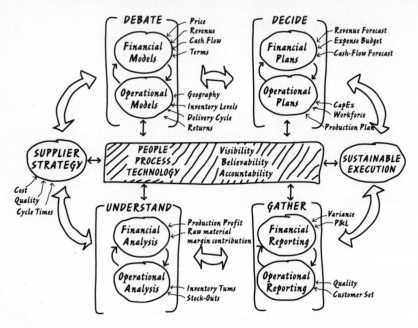

Figure 7.5   Full Supplier Performance Management Operating System
Source: Originally appeared in the December 2008 edition of Supply Chain Executive Magazine. Reprinted with permission.

and developers make to execute on the plan (which was based on the models that were based on the strategy). It includes financial plans such as revenue forecast (by product and/or by geography and/or by day/week/month), expense and cost-of-goods-sold budgets, cash-flow forecast, and other plans. It also includes operational plans such as your production plan, materials purchasing plan, workforce plan, and even your capital expenditure plan.

Having a systematic debate that informs your decision helps prevent the institutional amnesia that occurs when results aren't delivered as expected and senior management asks why the bar was set too high or too low. When plans are consolidated from each function and each business unit around the company, more constraints and assumptions are uncovered—and those should be fed back into the models so that the next model (next week, next month, next quarter) is even better than before.

While you are busy buying materials and services from suppliers, making products and services, and delivering to customers, you continually gather information about the business. This includes financial and operational reporting such as management reporting, product quality reporting, vendor-managed inventory reports, third-party logistics (3PL) reports, customer satisfaction reporting, and so on. This involves taking the raw transactional data (purchase orders, invoices, bills of lading) and turning them into useful, actionable information.

Once we have gathered believable information (by "believable," we refer to high data quality and common definitions and rules), we want to understand why we got the results we got. If we are spending more with one supplier than expected, what was the cause? Could it be we needed more raw materials or more finished-goods storage than we expected, and if so, what was the cause? Did we do a poor job of forecasting demand? Did we have a pricing promotion that production didn't know about? We want to get to the root causes of variances and problems—also known as "surprises"—and take action to fix them now and prevent them from happening in the future.

Most businesses are doing some form of each of these processes today. And they generally do them in silos: Manufacturing has its direct relationships with suppliers, while procurement is brought in to work on contracts; HR isn't often brought in for manufacturing staffing issues until the need is "right now" or until contract labor overtime is too burdensome; and sometimes different parts of the business use the same vendors under different contracts without leveraging them for better prices and terms. By using different technologies, unshared data, and business rules, with low or no sharing and collaboration across all four areas of the framework—not to mention low or no alignment with strategy—companies get low visibility into supplier performance, low believability in the numbers, and low accountability for results and corresponding actions. Supplier performance management is about bringing together all of the Gather, Understand, Debate, and Commit processes, technology, and people into a unified system.

Why Does Unified Sales Performance Management Matter?

The best way to illustrate the business benefit of a unified supplier performance management system is to show the potential financial impact on a company. Let's look at a case study using the computer hardware industry.

I picked Lenovo Group as our target company. Lenovo is the largest IT enterprise in China and acquired IBM's Personal Computing Division in 2005. The company manufactures and distributes brands such as ThinkPad and has manufacturing, distribution and support clusters in Raleigh, N.C., Beijing, Mexico, Brazil, Scotland, Hungary, India, Japan, Australia, and Singapore. I benchmarked Lenovo to the following competitors:

- Apple, Inc.
- Dell
- Gateway

Company	COG S	DPO
Lenovo Group	85.50%	−62
Apple, Inc.	64.50%	−56
Dell	80.70%	−67
Gateway	93.70%	−58
Industry Top 2%	68.50%	−49

Figure 7.6   Financial Impact of Supplier Performance Management on a Company

Source: Originally appeared in the December 2008 edition of Supply Chain Executive Magazine. Reprinted with permission.

Using only publicly available generally accepted accounting procedures (GAAP) data for the last four quarters for each company, I looked at a variety of results and focused in on two: COGS as a percentage of revenue, and DPO as shown in Figure 7.6.

For cost of goods sold as a percentage of revenue, where a lower percentage means they spend less on raw materials and on the design, manufacture and distribution of products, Lenovo Group ranks fourth out of five. For days payable outstanding, an indicator of how long a company is taking to pay its vendors and other trade creditors, they were second out of five (longer is generally—but not always—better for DPO, since the company can earn on the cash it owes trade creditors).

With only a 2% improvement in COGS and a 2% improvement in DPO, these incremental improvements would produce $167.7 million in cash as well as $239.7 million in recurring benefits for Lenovo. And we know 2% is possible in their industry since the competition is achieving results beyond 2%. So how can supplier performance management impact COGS and DPO by 2%?

To start, one of Lenovo's strategic objectives is to pursue operational excellence, which is about streamlining and improving their global supply chain and logistics network. Some of the initiatives already undertaken to improve the supply chain include:

- Operating its own facilities closer to their customer base in key geographies
- Expanding the reach and impact of its Lean Six Sigma application within the global supply chain; and
- Continuing to improve its logistics network

Some of the potential initiatives around supplier performance management, using the framework described earlier, that can have a direct impact

Table 7.2 Potential EPM Initiatives for Lenovo Group

	Cost of Goods Sold	Days Payable Outstanding
DEBATE		
Financial Models	Supplier M&A, joint-venture investment models	Variable supplier terms based on performance/geography
Operational Models	Model/SKU rationalization, harmonization	Supplier consolidation/distribution models
COMMIT		
Financial Plans	Internal forecast accuracy	Supplier forecast accuracy
Operational Plans	Materials management planning	Connecting contract labor suppliers to overtime forecasting
GATHER		
Financial Reporting	Product profitability reporting	3PL service level agreement variance reporting
Operational Reporting	Connecting suppliers to demand management reporting	Vendor invoice accuracy reports
UNDERSTAND		
Financial Analytics	Material cost analysis	Supplier cost benchmark analysis
Operational Analytics	Product transition process analysis	Supplier delivery cycle time analysis

Source: Originally appeared in the December 2008 edition of Supply Chain Executive Magazine. *Reprinted with permission.*

on the cost of goods sold and/or days payable outstanding, include those in Table 7.2.

Any combination of those initiatives could potentially improve COGS and DPO by at least 2% by giving Lenovo better visibility, believability, and accountability into supplier performance. And an investment in improving those processes and technologies is worth $167.7 million in cash, not to mention the recurring financial benefit.

Marketing Performance Management

Here are the management cycle components for a name-brand consumer goods company that engages in the design, marketing, and distribution of lifestyle products including apparel, accessories, leather goods, and home products.

Strategic objectives

- Brand: build and extend the brand
- Focus on specialty retail
- Expand international presence
- Continue cost-management efforts

Debate

- Financial models
  - Investment money
  - Store
  - Market
  - Working capital
  - Raw materials money
  - License acquisitions
  - Brand acquisitions/adjacencies
  - Price
  - Long-term profit and loss, balance sheet, cash flow
- Operational models
  - New product/category introductions
  - Volume
  - Capacity (factory, transportation)
  - Number of store openings/closings/renovations
  - Merchandise mix
  - Market share/percent expansion
  - Inventory growth/timing (by brand, by region, by channel, by season, by SKU)

Commit

- Financial plans
  - Sales plan
  - Revenue and expense plan
  - Marketing plan
  - CAPEX plan
- Operational plans
  - Store plans
  - Inventory plans

- Production plans
- Demand plans
- Workforce plan

Execute

- Areas of the business
  - Retail
  - Wholesale
  - Licensing
  - eCommerce
  - Design
  - Production
  - Merchandising
  - In-store presence

Gather

- Key financial reports
  - P&L by brand, comparable store, geography, channel
  - Comparable store sales
  - Returns, discounts, markdowns
- Key operational reports
  - Customer satisfaction survey report
  - Consolidated inventory report
  - Overtime reports

Understand

- Financial analytics
  - Brand/product profitability
  - Return on Marketing Investment (ROMI)
  - Store Profitability
  - Comparable Store Sales Trends
  - COGS Trends
  - DSO Trends
- Operational analytics
  - Productivity gains on incremental distribution
  - Conversion rates
  - Sell through rates by customer type, by price point
  - On-time delivery
  - Forecast accuracy

The Middle

- Master data management
  - Of product
  - Of accounts (chart of accounts)
  - Of store/geography

For this business, marketing performance management means continuously improving marketing effectiveness while delivering on as many strategic objectives and targets as possible.

For many years, there was a mad scramble at quarter-end to see how the sales forecast was shaping up. If the sales targets overachieved, additional discretionary funds were released to the corporate marketing department to spend at the end of the quarter for more print and web ad placements. This last-minute buying meant that ads were more expensive due to lack of lead time and pricing negotiation.

With a new EPM process in place, the company had more visibility into the sales, revenue, and expense forecast—including an assessment of forecast accuracy and probability—that allowed marketing to get more lead time on end-of-quarter investments. ROMI went up and advertising volume went up, meaning overall costs were reduced and the brand was strengthened (as

Table 7.3   EPM Components by Business Impact Area and Decision

	Revenue Growth	Operating Margin	Cash Cycle	Asset Utilization	EPM Tool/ Process
GATHER	P&L variance reporting	Customer/ product profitability dashboard	DSO, DPO, DII Dashboard	Downtime dashboards and reporting	Management reporting Statutory reporting dashboard
UNDER-STAND	Sales by channel trends Same store sales	Brand profitability	Inventory turns	3PL efficiency (on-time delivery)	Financial and operational analytics scorecard
DEBATE	Store expansion rate models	Headcount scenarios	Receivable collection acceleration models	Capacity planning	Financial and Operational modeling Predictive analytics
COMMIT	Weekly sales forecast	Annual operating plan	Collections forecasting	CAPEX planning	Budgeting, planning and forecasting

Table 7.4   EPM Initiatives by Industry by Management Process

	Industry					
	Banking	**Insurance**	**Health care**	**Retail**	**Energy**	**High Tech**
GATHER	Retail branch profitability reporting Noninterest income by product and segment Compliance and disclosure (Basel II)	Claims management reporting Claims executive dashboard Profitability reporting	Compliance scorecard Departmental P&L Fraud and abuse reporting	Category management Store performance reporting Loss/shrink alerting	Site operations dashboard Variance reports and alerts Site and shift rankings	Employee skill reporting Product P&L Customer satisfaction dashboard
UNDERSTAND	Product profitability analysis Pricing behavior/hyper-segmentation Credit risk analysis	Straight-through processing analysis Claims procurement analysis Claim value chain analysis	Accounts receivable analysis Patient lifecycle analysis Diagnosis Related Group (DRG) analysis	Customer segmentation Item profitability Stock-out analysis Campaign and loyalty analysis	Cost applicable to sales analysis Global procurement trends Efficiency analysis	Sales cycle time analysis Employee turnover trends Marketing campaign effectiveness
DEBATE	Household pricing alternatives M&A Models Customer segmentation scenarios	Risk scenarios Underwriting models Distribution efficiency models	Pricing alternatives Preventative care modeling M&A models	Pricing alternatives New store openings Promotion models	Acquisition model Debt modeling Price (in and out) modeling	Product/price mix model M&A models Debt modeling
COMMIT	Channel forecast Event campaign planning Relationship forecast	Line of business P&L Forecast Channel planning Agent Workforce planning	Reimbursement planning Capital expenditure planning Workforce planning	Price and promotion planning Merchandise planning Workforce planning	Production forecast Capacity planning Capital expense planning	Revenue and expense forecast by product Workforce planning Channel forecast

measured by unaided awareness)—two of the key strategic objectives for the company.

Summary

Table 7.3 takes a quick look at how EPM initiatives can be aligned to each stage of the management cycle, and each area of strategic objectives and outcomes.

There is almost no limit on the number of EPM initiatives that can be designed and developed which can have a positive impact on the business. Table 7.4 shows some industry-specific EPM initiatives organized by management decision step.

By the time you get to the end of Chapter 9, you should see how you'll be able to identify the top EPM initiatives in your organization that help build out your EPM roadmap.

Notes

1. Adapted from Barry Trailer and Jim Dickie, "Understanding What Your Sales Manager Is Up Against," *Harvard Business Review*, July–August 2006.
2. This section, "Supply Chain Performance Management," originally appeared in *Supply Chain Executive Magazine*, December 2008. Ron Dimon and Simon Tucker, Reprinted with permission.

CHAPTER 8

Strategy: Aligned to the Right Outcomes

> However beautiful the strategy, you should occasionally look at the results.
>
> —WINSTON CHURCHILL

So far we've covered how the management operating system helps validate organizational strategy by testing the objectives through a series of financial and operational what-if models (Chapter 5), which are fed by facts uncovered from actual and variance data (Chapter 4). More often than not, that turns out to be a "snapshot" or health-check type of exercise, done once during the corporate strategic planning cycle, or done quarterly to true-up the objectives. However, EPM helps make this strategy alignment an ongoing process. It can help organizations be more flexible and responsive in strategy setting, strategy execution, and the overall business model. This chapter will explore the strategy components of the management operating system and exactly how EPM helps align the entire organization to the "right" outcomes.

The Language of Strategy

It's useful to take a minute and differentiate some of the components that make up a company strategy:

- **Mission.** The purpose of the organization
- **Vision.** An aspirational, conceptual future state of the organization
- **Values.** Overall organizational priorities that are aligned with the mission and vision
- **Goals.** Measurable end results that support the mission and vision and are compatible with the values. Goals are usually longer term, and have a specific time-frame, for example "three to five years."

- **Objectives.** Specific activities with outcomes that support the goals (usually shorter term).
- **Corporate Strategy.** According to Michael Porter, corporate strategy is about competitive differentiation: deliberately choosing a different set of activities to deliver a unique mix of value.[1] Your definition of strategy may differ, and that's okay, so long as your senior management team agrees on that definition. For further reading on the subject, I highly recommend *Strategy Safari: A Guided Tour Through the Wilds of Strategic Management* by Henry Mintzberg et al.
- **Marketing Strategy.** How and when marketing resources, including pricing, products, promotion, and place (the "4 P's"), will be deployed in support of the overall corporate strategy.
- **Sales Strategy.** The approach to account management, lead identification, qualification, and conversion to support the organization's sales quotas or targets.

And so on through each business function—how they will approach supporting the company strategic objectives that they own, contribute directly to, or can influence.

While each functional leader, CMO, CIO, CFO, and so on, will define their functional strategy, they have to align with the overall company strategy, or, better yet, be integrated into one holistic organizational strategy. In this chapter, we'll look at how this is done in the management operating system and how EPM supports the development and alignment of the holistic strategy.

Functional Value Maps

The traditional approach to holistic strategy description is through Strategy Maps popularized by Kaplan & Norton.[2] These are organized by the four perspectives of the Balanced Scorecard:

1. Financial
2. Customer
3. Internal processes
4. Learning and growth

Figure 8.1 is a good example of a strategy map showing loose connections among each of the perspectives all the way up to long-term shareholder value and somewhat divided into a two strategies: productivity (left-hand side) and growth (right-hand side).

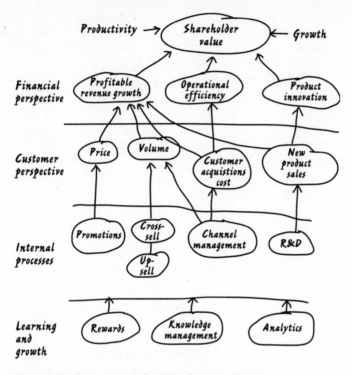

Figure 8.1   Strategy Map for Manufacturing Business

Functional value maps take the four (or more) balanced perspectives and map them into the organization structure of the business. This gives more clarity around accountability, ownership, and consumption. It makes a stronger case for removing information silos in an organization and promoting sharing and collaboration. It also shows potential drill-paths for root-cause analytics. Finally, it's a way to prioritize drivers for driver-based planning and metrics for reporting and analytics.

Functional value maps place the drivers of value in each business function according to which layer of the business owns the results, using a matrix like Table 2.1 from Chapter 2 and Figure 4.2 from Chapter 4, and then interconnects them to show cause-and-effect relationships. For example, using portions of the strategy map in Figure 8.1, a functional value map would look like Figure 8.2.

Now you can see how the strategic objectives are aligned to the key value drivers and among those you see which naturally prioritize based on the number of connections in and out. For example, notice the impact of customer acquisition at the intersection of Operations and Sales. This is

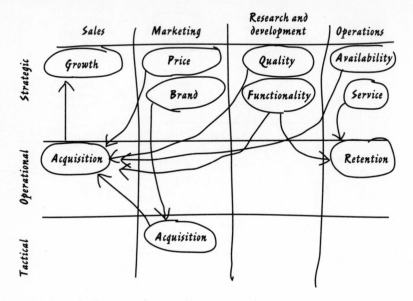

Figure 8.2   Functional Value Map based on the Strategy Map in Figure 8.1

where sales management is accountable for net-new clients and is distinct from customer acquisition at the tactical layer of marketing, which is where lead generation happens. So many drivers impact customer acquisition in sales, such as price, quality, functionality, leads, and so on, and it directly impacts sales growth—so it is a highly prioritized driver of value in the organization, yet it is practically buried in the strategy map. Having more visibility and accountability of customer acquisition rates and volumes would certainly be aligning the right outcomes to strategy. Of course prioritization is also governed by the materiality and volatility of the value driver, as mentioned in Chapter 2 in the Impact section. A high-impact approach to connecting EPM initiatives to strategic objectives is to run each high-priority value driver through the management operating system. This will be further explored in Chapter 9, in the Your EPM Roadmap section.

Optics: Line of Sight

Business optics is the practice of being able to see what matters in the business. It means visually digesting information in a way that helps guide you to new insights and helps you make better business decisions. Optics can include reports, scorecards, dashboards, alerts, and other data visualization tools. Ideally, optics are delivered to you in a way that fits your role in the organization. They should be:

- The right metrics
- At the right level of detail: from summarized to very granular
- At the right time: real-time, daily, monthly, etc.
- At the right periodicity: for example, daily sales delivered weekly
- Versus the right target: variance to plan, budget, forecast, benchmark, or other relevant target
- Having the right drill path: when you click on it, it takes you to the most relevant drivers and root-causes
- Having other qualifiers you may need to know: risk weighting, data-quality grade, "freshness date," and so on

Usually these qualities of data are packaged to appeal to certain roles in the organization. For example, an executive dashboard gets the "big button" look-and-feel with highly summarized, color-coded current results versus plan or versus prior period ("red is bad, green is good") and a large arrow showing trending ("up is good, down is bad"). A finance analyst gets a blank grid where she drags the dimensions to be analyzed into rows and columns and "slices and dices" interactively until a result, insight, or root cause is revealed. You want people at all levels of the organization to be able to see how what they are working on contributes to overall success. So optics for an accounts receivable clerk would show how aged receivables impacts days sales outstanding which impacts working capital and free cash flow.

While optics are relevant for your role in the organization, you may want to share your insight with a colleague or group of people to show them what you've discovered, persuade them to your point of view, justify a decision, or enroll them into an idea. Ideally, you want what you see to be easily seen by others and easily recreated in the future. Saving and sharing a particular view on data is important; however it's just as important to be able to convey the context of that view along with the view.

As with any business system or process, there are traps to be avoided, including:

- Skewed or misleading views: perhaps only sales from the last week of the quarter are used to show sales-rep productivity, while showing the entire quarter gives a different picture
- Nonsense views: showing accounts receivable balances compared to travel and entertainment expenses may not yield any insights
- Distracting views: monitoring the number of Web hits may not be the best use of time for a product development manager

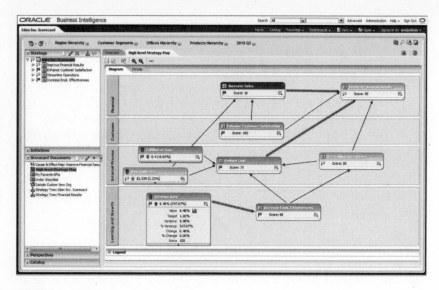

Figure 8.3   Balanced Scorecard System.
Courtesy Oracle Corp.

- Measuring the wrong things: monitoring metrics simply because the data is available (conversely not monitoring the right metrics because the data is not available), monitoring metrics because that's the way you've always done it, or not questioning what you measure

Balanced scorecards are a good example of management-level optics. Figure 8.3 shows a typical Balanced Scorecard screenshot showing traceability from drivers at different levels (perspectives) to the overall goals, one of which is Improve Financial Results in this case.

Metrics Equal Focus

Why do you need more focus? Because of change. As the market, the economy, technology, our customers, and our competitors all change, so must you. We can look at all the different areas of change:

- **Speed.** Things are getting faster, like business cycles, time to market, and logistics.
- **Volume.** In some areas more is being demanded and produced, and in other areas, less.

- **Resilience.** We want to protect market share, customer loyalty, intellectual property.
- **Quality.** As customers become smarter, and competition increases, we have to make products better, train people more.
- **Impact.** More transparency is demanded, concerns for community and the environment have become customer buying criteria.
- **Cost.** The flatter world has given us cheaper labor, competition can drive down price, and global shortages can erode margin.

"EPM done right" means having a focus on the most important levers, or value drivers, in your organization. It means paying attention to what matters.

Metrics are not only reporting objects, they are also the drivers of driver-based planning—they have targets, owners; they are the levers of the business that you pull in order to move the right performance needle.

There is still some debate as to the definitions of a measure, a metric, a key performance driver (KPD), a key value driver (KVD), and a key performance indicator (KPI). I generally go with the following: a metric is a type of measure, usually reserved for business activities, and a KPI is more closely tied to the strategy of the business and includes comparison to a target. And to avoid the debate altogether, I generally talk about "what drives value." In that way, I don't actually care if something is a measure, metric, KPI, lever, or so on—I care that that thing helps drive value in the business. So in a "metrics" discovery session with business users, I will record value-drivers and later, when designing a solution with IT professionals, I'll get into the metrics, measures, and KPIs.

Metrics can be:

- Financial/operational/strategic
- Internal/external
- Tangible/intangible
- Short term/long term
- Leading/lagging (although a case can usually be made for many metrics to be both)

As discussed throughout this book, their relative importance is guided by:

- Materiality
- Volatility
- Proximity to strategic objectives
- Alignment through the value chain to the strategic objective
- Number of connections to other value drivers
- "Popularity"—meaning number of times it's used, mentioned, asked for

It's also useful to keep in mind that there are "meat and potatoes" metrics —a steady diet that gives you a basis for year-over-year comparison and trends. These you try to keep standard so you can compare apples to apples—unless the business changes dramatically and makes the metric irrelevant. And then there are the "soup du jour" metric—a series of changing yet important metrics that help bring attention and focus to issues and initiatives of the day (or the month or quarter). One meat and potatoes metric that rarely goes away—although how it gets calculated may change—is profitability.

Profitability

Almost every commercial organization I have served has had some element of profitability as part of their strategic objectives. Some simply declare "profitable revenue growth" as their objective; others might be more specific and call out components of overall profitability, including:

- Customer profitability (this can be named customer, customer industry, or customer type)
- Product profitability
- Channel profitability
- Market profitability (this can be geographic or demographic)
- Seasonal profitability

Yet it is still a challenge to many organizations to accurately measure profitability. Part of the problem has been identifying and applying the best cost allocation methodology as discussed in Chapter 3, in the Management and Statutory Reporting section. But once you have solved that concern and begin to track profitability by the dimensions that make sense for your business, then what? What actions would you be willing to take when you know what your profitability is?

The process of calculating and exposing profitability should connect directly to your strategic objectives. It should also help you articulate your business model, tolerances, and standard operating procedures around profit.

Table 8.1 shows some example strategic decisions that have been made once true profitability has been included in the management operating system.

EPM is the perfect environment for managing profitability: you take profitability through the entire management operating system and debate it: What's a possible stretch goal for overall profitability? And what would the working capital and headcount requirements be to achieve it? Once the best scenario is selected, the modeled components generate the expense plan, revenue plan, headcount plan, and capital expenditure (CAPEX) plans—where all levels of the organization are held accountable to their commitments. As

Table 8.1   Actions That Can Impact Profitability

Profitability Component	Strategy Impact
Customer profitability	Fire your most unprofitable customers Start tracking customer lifetime value, offer new incentives
Product profitability	Declare deliberate loss-leaders, develop new bundles Revise pricing strategy
Channel profitability	Offer free training to the channel Segment marketing promotions differently (e.g., let the indirect channel own small/medium size enterprises where the cost of sales does not support the price point)
Market profitability	Invest in new markets Exit unprofitable mature markets
Seasonal profitability	Tune staffing plans Tune working capital and inventory plans

you execute the plans you keep your eye on all dimensions of profitability and get alerted to customers, products, channels, markets, and weeks that miss the target or the profitability tolerance. Then you drill into the root cause to understand the miss and act accordingly: redeploy resources, revise targets, and revisit assumptions and constraints. Depending on the impact of the miss, you go back to the debate, see what's changed, and adapt to new realities and declare what's next. Once you start seeing repeating profitability patterns, you have a new debate—one that could lead you to alter your strategy.

Strategic Flexibility

One of the keys to growth is maintaining strategic flexibility: not being rigidly tied to goals that were set in one set of circumstances, using one set of assumptions, when those circumstances have changed. According to William Duggan in his book *Strategic Intuition*, instead of setting goals first, you are well advised to watch for large-payoff/low-cost opportunities first and then set goals.[3] In an EPM world, you would have those opportunity models ready at hand and ready to turn into operating and financial execution plans.

One way to use the EPM model to accomplish this is with a rigorous debate in the business about future scenarios. This includes capturing financial and operational models based on possible futures. For example, having a complete set of financial statement models (including cash flow) that includes a variety of assumptions about the following drivers:

- Competitive landscape (a "Coke/Pepsi" scenario could show what would happen if your two biggest competitors merged, market by market).

- Customer retention (the "Mattel" scenario could show what the P&L would look like if there was a massive product recall in your industry).
- Economic shift (your "Merrill Lynch" scenario would show what would happen to cost of capital and profitability should there be a rapid downturn in the credit markets).
- Rapid new product innovation (your "Apple" scenario would show predicted revenue and margin growth should your new product get to market faster and enjoy accelerated brand recognition).

Just going through the process of creating these models—in a holistic enterprise way, not just by an analyst in finance—will create some useful debate in the business on where resources are best deployed and which model yields the best returns. Hatch and Zweig published a paper in 2001 that is still relevant today.[4]

They say that the ability to effect strategic change is a result of:

1. Entertaining multiple options
2. Improving competitive intelligence
3. Improving the customer experience
4. Improving the employee experience
5. Maintaining the appropriate level of overhead
6. Flexible systems and processes
7. Few decision-makers at the top

Each of these levers can be modeled, planned-for, reported on, and analyzed in an EPM framework. Employees at all levels can share and collaborate on their creation, have visibility into results and variance, and mine for new insights and opportunities.

Closing the Gap

Let's go back to the management cycle and take a look at how strategy relates to the Debate and Understand processes. In Figure 8.4, we see a two-way arrow from Strategy to Debate, and a two-way arrow from Strategy to Understand.

The arrow from Strategy into Debate tells us that the strategic objectives are what lead the debate. If the objective is 5% year-over-year revenue growth, the debate includes a model of sales, customers, headcount, new products, economic indicators, and so on. If your model tells us it's not possible to achieve that level of growth knowing what you know, the arrow points back to strategy: You may have to revise your objectives—or at least your targets.

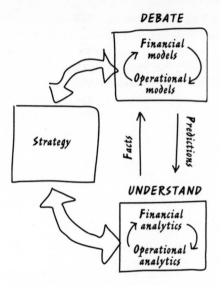

Figure 8.4 ⁄ Strategy in the
Management Operating System

Conversely, if your model tells you that 7% is not only possible, but quite probable, then you update your strategy accordingly.

The arrow from Strategy to Understand tells us that when we are formulating or revising our strategy, we want to go back into an analysis of the facts to support our direction and objectives. For example, let's look at a trend of sales, costs, average selling price, volume, market size, and so on, and look for patterns that support our strategy. Likewise, while doing our analyses to understand the business, we may have a unique opportunity to alter our strategy to take advantage of changing circumstances (e.g., we may notice a sustained spike in sales of a particular product line to a particular demographic, and revise our strategy to focus on that demographic).

The Debate and Understand EPM processes are adjacent to Strategy for a reason: They are there to help organizations be more flexible in direction and approach and base strategy on what's actually happening and on what's possible given the facts.

Summary

What if strategy was everyone's business? Instead of being handed down from on-high, what-if strategy formulation and execution were collaborative, fact-based processes that everyone had visibility to and could possibly make a contribution to? The management operating system addresses the gap between strategy and sustainable execution by asking "what's possible" or "what's next" and "why are we getting the results we're getting?" By questioning, modeling, and testing our assumptions, constraints, and drivers of value, we can continuously test our strategy collaboratively and transparently—and continuously get better at the strategy process itself. One of the keys is having visibility into what drives strategy, especially profitability. And then, once seen, determining what to do about it and assigning responsibility and accountability to the results.

Notes

1. Michael Porter, *Competitive Strategy: Techniques for Analyzing Industries and Competitors*, Free Press, 1998.
2. Robert Kaplan and David Norton, *Strategy Maps: Converting Intangible Assets into Tangible Outcomes*, Harvard Business Review Press, 2004.
3. William Duggan, *Strategic Intuition: The Creative Spark in Human Achievement*, Columbia University Press, 2007.
4. Jim Hatch and Jeffrey Zweig, March/April 2001, "Strategic Flexibility—The Key to Growth," www.iveybusinessjournal.com/topics/strategy/strategic-flexibility-the-key-to-growth#. UKVOhYUmRt4, retrieved November 16, 2012.

CHAPTER 9

Bringing It All Together

Organizations that have implemented Performance Management more broadly are nearly four times more likely to be among the most competitive organizations in their industry.

—Brian McDonough
Research Manager, Analytics and Data Warehousing Software, IDC,
Financial Performance and Strategy Management Survey
of Buyer Priorities for 2011, Doc #226261, Dec. 2010

EPM done right is really about bringing together all those EPM-like components that you probably already do in silos, in part, in spreadsheets, or are hoping to do if you had the time. It's about bringing together:

- Modeling, planning, reporting, and analytics
- Finance and Operations
- Strategy and execution
- Data, master data, and information
- Rules and definitions
- The past, the present, and the future
- Decisions, actions, and results

The culmination of these components, working together, is the EPM management operating system cycle and has been the framework for this book. The cycle is shown in its entirety in Figure 9.1.

Just like EPM is bringing together all those components of the management operating system, Chapter 9 is about bringing together the concepts and practices of EPM done right.

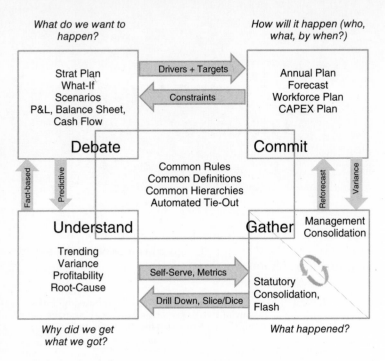

Figure 9.1   The EPM Management Operating System

Alignment

The Random House Unabridged Dictionary[1] defines alignment as "a state of agreement or cooperation among persons, groups, etc., with a common cause or viewpoint." It's easy to see how EPM enables this "state." Ideally, EPM provides an environment of cooperation (for purposes of modeling, planning, and reporting and analysis), which supports agreement (one version of the truth) among the various persons and groups within the organization. And it helps those users take action in pursuit of their "common cause": achieving performance targets, executing company strategy, and delivering value to stakeholders.

But EPM doesn't just enable alignment; it also demands it. Alignment is one ingredient that's critical to success if you want to use EPM to help you execute on your strategy, survive these difficult times, and be fully prepared to emerge in a stronger position when the economy recovers. You can have the most advanced technical infrastructure, the latest business process management (BPM) tools, pristine data, executive sponsorship, and well-defined EPM processes, but unless these are financially and operationally aligned—across functions and through all layers of the business—with your organizational ecosystem and your overarching strategy, you won't achieve the best return on your EPM investment.

Business/IT Alignment

Harvard Business Review advocates that business and IT shouldn't just be aligned, they should be "forged together."[2] One way the authors say you can do this is by having the CIO report directly to the CEO or COO, not the CFO. While we have seen this reporting structure in many of our client organizations, it does not automatically mean that IT and the business are forged together, or even aligned for that matter.

Certainly the business analyst (BA) role has done much for crossing the chasm, in both directions, for IT and the business. And where we see the most successful financial systems implementations are where the finance/information systems (IS) role acts as the BA. But this is still not a guarantee for a meeting of the minds between business and IT.

I propose five "better" practices for closer IT/business alignment based on my client engagements over the last 30 years.

1. **Start with corporate strategy and objectives.** It sounds all well and good, but many IT organizations miss this. We must directly correlate any and all IT initiatives with the overall corporate strategy. IT should be able to show a "drill path" from strategy, through objectives, into initiatives and on to metrics and data. For example, let's say your company objective is 15% year-over-year profitable revenue growth. This is a meaty one with several parts:

   - Revenue growth (sell more stuff)
   - Profitable revenue growth (sell more stuff and make money doing it)
   - Continuous profitable revenue growth (do the same year-over-year)

   So how does one or more (hopefully many) IT initiatives help promote selling, product expansion, reducing cost of goods, and supporting a pipeline of innovation to feed future years? If you show multiple correlations from many systems to many strategic objectives, you are more aligned.

2. **Take a holistic view.** Usually, one part of the business, a function such as Marketing, Operations, or HR, comes to IT with a business problem to solve. For example, Sales would ask, "We need more visibility into customer profitability to find out if any customers are costing us money." It is IT's job to take the enterprise-wide view of this problem. Who else needs to see this information (Customer Support, Product Development, Marketing)? How will this information be made "actionable" so we can watch trends over time, adjust for

seasonality, compare with forecasts, and eventually fire our unprofitable customers? When Sales approaches IT, IT takes the request as an enterprise request, not a Sales request.

3. **Highlight the requirements gap.** IT organizations usually do a very good job of gathering user requirements, data models, source system availability, and so on. These are bottom-up requirements. Many times we see a lack of insight into top-down requirements: What are the line-of-business owners and functional executives looking for? Business/IT alignment happens when the BA looks into the gap between bottom-up and top-down. We did a large enterprise-wide financial system implementation for a Fortune 500 holding company—it was grueling, but in the end it worked according to spec and added tremendous value to the company (it had a net positive impact on earnings per share [EPS]). When we went to the CFO to tell him we were in production, he wanted to know where his spend-analysis was. This was never in the spec. Big gap, low alignment.

4. **Have a long-term roadmap into which short-term initiatives fit.** Designing, building, and rolling out systems (and processes for that matter), without a long-term IT roadmap is a recipe for more information silos, more redundant systems, more extract, transform, load (ETL) complexity, and so on. The roadmap should make some simple distinctions, such as the layers of information-value in the organization, for example (top-down):

- Knowledge
- Actionable information
- Value-added information (and business rules)
- Consolidated, summarized, hierarchical master data
- Transformed data
- Operational data (or data warehouse)
- Transactional data

It should also layer applications in the overall system architecture, such as:

- Information delivery/Front-end apps
- Value-added apps
- Information gathering/Operational apps
- Transactional apps/Real-time apps

The management operating system described in this book is a guiding business process framework onto which you can hang your IT roadmap and portfolio of initiatives.

5. **Accountability.** The final "better" practice I'll share has to do with accountability. This is the idea of making sure all levels and all functions of the business are working on their part of executing the

corporate strategy. How do I know, as an accounts receivable (A/R) clerk for example, how what I am doing impacts profitable revenue growth? IT systems should be tailored for the appropriate intersection of layer and function (tactical finance in this case) in an organization and should come with visibility and insight into my contribution. Without that (and a public measurement system), there will be low or no enterprise accountability.

How do you prioritize your IT portfolio of initiatives in this economy?

If you're like most enterprises, you have a backlog of IT initiatives lined up on the heels of your work in progress (WIP). You may also have some new pressure to take a harder look at costs and potentially trim or reprioritize your WIP and your backlog.

So how do you decide what stays and what gets put on hold (or cancelled)? And for what stays, how do you reorder your efforts to make sure IT is delivering the best return on investment?

As I mention a bit further on in this chapter, return on investment (ROI) (including total cost of ownership [TCO]) analysis is a good acid test for IT projects, but it's not the only ingredient nor the primary consideration for green-lighting or keeping an initiative—especially a strategic systems initiative (one that will give you a competitive advantage in the market).

Here are some of those other ingredients that you should use:

1. **Show how the initiative helps drive strategic objectives.** Drive is the operative word here. Many systems will help you measure strategic objectives—Balanced Scorecards for instance—but they may not pass the "so what" test. You have to not only measure the objective, but also analyze why the measurement came out the way it did (cause and effect) *and* update your models and scenarios with that new learning *and* flow that into your revised or rolling forecasts, ultimately helping managers make a decision and take some action that will move you closer to the objective.

2. **Show the materiality of the initiative.** Priority should be given to those initiatives that have the most material impact on the business. You could be working on a reporting rationalization and consolidation initiative that would save the company 5% of selling, general, and administrative (SG&A) expense—great stuff! But if you also had an initiative on deck to show product, customer, and channel profitability that would allow sales and marketing managers to sell more profitable products and services as well as cross-sell and up-sell that would increase revenue growth by 5%, which would have a higher priority? (This is a trick question, by the way—the CFO will have you do both! Hopefully this will displace projects that aren't as material).

3. **Show how the initiative improves visibility into the business and collaboration across business functions.** Among other things, organizational effectiveness is grounded in fact-based decisions, accountability for those decisions (and results), and every person having line of site that shows how what they are working on impacts the bottom-line. Breaking down functional silos is key to improving collaboration and sharing of information—if your initiative can improve visibility and collaboration, it will probably lead to number 1 and number 2.

Finally, looking at the management operation system in Figure 9.1 I have noticed that "the business" (operations, sales and marketing, production) generally starts from the left side, from strategic objectives into the Debate and Understand areas, IT starts from the right side (tactical execution, transactional systems) into Gather, and Finance usually lives in the middle (it "owns" the numbers) and the Commit areas. So the management operating system cycle is a good way to bring together all parties in an organization to agree on improving performance.

Strategy/Operations/Tactical Alignment

How do you know whether people at all levels of the organization are working in unison towards strategic objectives? And how do they know if they are on track? The need for a clear drill path from day-to-day activities and outcomes to strategy is a key tenet in enterprise accountability. If you're an A/R clerk and you can easily see the impact of days sales outstanding (DSO) on corporate cash flow or on investors' valuation of the company, you are more likely to want to improve that measure. And if company leaders want to drive more of that behavior, they can connect bonuses to job-specific measures and targets.

An EPM scorecard or dashboard is the perfect way to monitor alignment up and down the organization. The built-in ability of EPM systems to work with a variety of hierarchies helps you to see how the business rolls up from different perspectives: by entity, by geography, by product line, or by chart of accounts. From the bottom up, our A/R clerk gets to see the value of his or her contribution. From the top down, executives get to see the most material contributors to, and detractors from, results.

Amazingly, many companies don't know which measures truly drive value in the business. They can't answer the simple question: What are the key drivers (key performance indicators [KPIs], metrics, etc.) that have the biggest material impact on strategic objectives?

For example, we once worked with a high-tech client in Silicon Valley. We interviewed all of the top executives and senior leaders in this 4,000-employee organization to determine the most important drivers of value. We talked to the CEO, the COO, the executive vice president of sales, the vice president of HR, and even the chairman of the board. We expected that the consensus would identify such measures as profitable and sustainable revenue growth, high operating margins, or customer satisfaction.

But it turned out that the primary driver of value was employee skills. Employees with advanced degrees, professional certifications, and industry experience were the key generator of value for this organization. They kept the customers happy, they developed superior products, and they captured revenue.

Yet this company didn't have a single measure around employee skills. Management didn't capture that information, or even plan for it in the budget.

Recognizing this anomaly was an enlightening experience for the company's leadership. If they wanted to put their money where their mouth was—and put some meaning behind statements like "people are our most important asset"—they would have to create measures for employee skills and build them into their models, forecasts, and management reporting and analysis processes and systems.

Doing so would not mean that they were giving HR too much say in the strategic planning process. After all, every function—including Operations, Marketing, Sales, and Development, and in the operating units as well as at corporate headquarters—clearly had a stake in actualizing the "people as assets" philosophy. Measuring and improving employee skills was vital to generating customer and stakeholder value.

And the initiative would need to be coordinated and companywide. As Robert S. Kaplan and David P. Norton note in their book *Alignment*, if a company wants to capture economies of scale and scope, "corporate headquarters needs a tool to articulate a theory for how to operate the multiple units within the corporate structure to create value beyond what the individual units could achieve on their own."[3]

Financial/Operational Alignment

Senior management creates targets based on financial measures—let's say, 10% year-over-year revenue growth. When these targets are delivered to the operations side of the business, they are quickly translated into operational targets (so many additional units at a certain price). The farther down into Operations you go, the more granular the drivers get; for example, more volume might mean more productivity, more work shifts, or more headcount. Once the operational results are in, managers have to translate them back into financial terms to communicate them to senior management. When this is done right, you can easily see the cause-and-effect relationship between operational drivers and financial results.

Most first-generation EPM initiatives do a good job of this translation in areas such as driver-based planning and operational business intelligence. But there's another area that I think is ripe for exploitation in the next generation of EPM initiatives: connecting the budgeting, planning and forecasting processes back to the financial and operational models that link strategy to plans. For example, when senior managers debate which objectives and targets are achievable, they should be able to record their assumptions, constraints, and drivers in an EPM tool with a governance (review and approval) process. The agreed-upon operational model, with its financial targets, then forms the basis of the annual operating plan and subsequent budgets. As plans and forecasts bubble up from the lower levels of the organization, new assumptions, constraints, and drivers will arise (new regional competitors may change the business outlook, for instance.) These can be fed back into the corporate operational model so that the next cycle is closely aligned with reality. As one of my clients put it, "Numbers drive dollars and dollars drive numbers."

Cross-Functional Alignment

Even though every function has a stake in a company's outcomes, many organizations underperform because critical information is trapped in silos. For example, if marketing launches a new promotion, sales needs to know the projected impact on leads, which then (depending on the sales conversion drivers) turns into sales and revenue. Manufacturing needs to know how much volume to expect so that it can update production schedules and alert suppliers that they may need to buy more raw materials. Finance needs to release working capital and prepare to extend more customer credit. It's not hard to imagine the disaster that might unfold if the marketing effort scores a big success, but the company can't deliver.

So a business needs to be horizontally event driven; it needs to understand how a course of action adopted by one function impacts other functions. This is a balancing act. In the previous example, let's say Finance declares that there won't be enough working capital available in the time needed for the sales projected. What does the business do now? Most likely, sales and marketing efforts will have to be scaled back to match capital availability.

EPM software supports horizontal alignment by giving the various corporate departments visibility into plans, actuals, and variances based on business goals rather than business functions. In the example, rather than relying on a marketing dashboard or a sales dashboard, the company might deploy a campaign-to-cash dashboard that could be accessed by marketing, sales, operations, and finance, all of which have a "common cause" and need to establish a "state of agreement and cooperation" for the initiative. EPM is the glue for that collaboration.

Internal/External Alignment

Many EPM-enabled businesses are tightly focused on alignment within their own four walls, but the ongoing evolution of EPM is enabling companies to extend modeling, planning, reporting, and analytics to the entire value chain. For example, you can use EPM to give customers and suppliers insight into your inventory and delivery times, and even your quality metrics. Alignment with the external ecosystem helps your company understand exactly what's important to the people you do business with.

Consider including external users in your EPM plans, especially in forecasting and business intelligence initiatives. We're seeing more and more activity and thought-leadership in this area. For example, Whole Foods recently announced plans to enable its suppliers and vendors to view sales data for their product lines through an EPM application. Many of our clients are opting to include suppliers and customers in the scope of our foundational requirements discovery method. As detailed in Chapter 7, a specialized area of EPM called supplier performance management is starting to emerge. And performance networks, which include all related parties in EPM, will be an important part of the next level of performance management.

A Common Business Language

When you interconnect all of the management operating system processes, you get "The Middle." The middle is where you can create a common business language through:

- Common data and metadata
- Common definitions, algorithms, and formulae
- Common hierarchies
- Common business rules
- Common security

By bringing together all of the components of EPM into one system, as shown in Figure 9.2, you get to improve the quality and believability of information coming out of transactional and analytical systems. You also get better control in that you can audit where numbers came from, how and when they were changed, and by whom. You could say that EPM governance lives in this middle.

Without this common ground, you will continue to have difficulties agreeing on the definitions of things instead of what to do about them. There are many organizations that don't have one definition of a customer, of sales, or even what constitutes a full-time equivalent employee. Think of EPM as

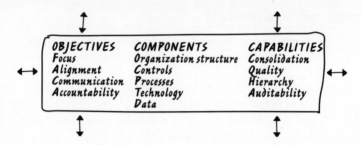

OBJECTIVES	COMPONENTS	CAPABILITIES
Focus	Organization structure	Consolidation
Alignment	Controls	Quality
Communication	Processes	Hierarchy
Accountability	Technology	Auditability
	Data	

Figure 9.2   The Middle of the Management Operating System

the new "middle management"—managing to the same focus, alignment, and accountability throughout the organization.

Let's look at Peter Drucker's summary of what managers do:

- Set objectives
- Allocate and organize resources
- Measure and communicate results
- Develop and motivate people[4]

This really has not changed that much in the fifty years since he wrote it. And this is not a "to-do" list. These are the components of an ongoing, closed-loop system that is designed to improve with every iteration. However, what motivates people at work is changing. Taking liberties with Daniel Pink's assertion of what motivates us at work, EPM can directly support employee engagement:[5]

1. **Autonomy.** EPM systems let you act more autonomously by making fact-based decisions and having more transparent access to targets, plans, and results.
2. **Mastery.** Mastering "the great game of business"[6] needs visibility into how things work and accountability of my part of the whole.
3. **Purpose.** Everything comes back to mission, vision, value, and strategy. EPM lets me see how what I do has an impact on what the organization is up to.

Along these lines, some say that a results-only work environment (ROWE) gives the same sense of autonomy, mastery, and purpose. Where better to design, track, and deliver results than EPM?

EPM is a discipline that lets managers manage the business and helps all members of an organization speak the same language and motivate themselves to deliver performance.

Maturity Is in the Arrows

In August 2012, I helped organize an EPM user forum in Chicago where Finance and IT attendees from 25 companies were represented. All of these companies had implemented parts of the management operating system and represent the complete spectrum of EPM maturity. I took the opportunity to do a survey of EPM usage across the entire management operating system of 88 finance and IT EPM practitioners, and I organized the results into three company sizes based on annual revenue (small = < $100 million, medium = $100 million to $1 billion, large = > $1 billion).

The survey itself (see Figure 9.3) took a bit of time to explain, and I had presented the management operating system to the group so the diagram would mean something to them.

After a couple of questions and answers it got sorted out. The results were very interesting to me. Here's what the survey completed by one organization (over $1 billion in annual revenue) in Figure 9.3 says:

- Modeling, 3/10. "We don't do 'what-if' modeling very well and we really need it."

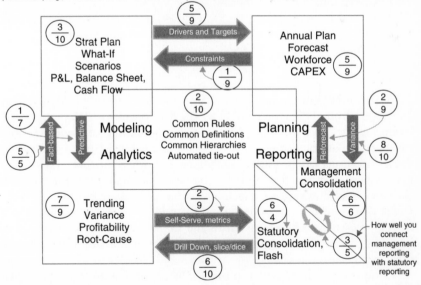

EPM Cycle Survey: In each circle, enter a numerator (top number) of how well you do the thing—on a scale of 1 (don't do it) to 10 (do it very well), and enter a denominator (bottom number) of how much you need the thing—on a scale of 1 (don't need it) to 10 (must have it). E.g., 1/10 means we don't do it and we really need it, 8/2 means we're pretty good at it, but don't need it that much.

Figure 9.3   Completed Management Operating System Survey, August 2012

- Drivers/targets, 5/9. "We're not bad, we do some driver-based planning and we have targets for most things, and it's a very important to get better at this."
- Constraints, 1/9. "Learning from our planning and analysis processes, and feeding-back constraints into our models would make a big difference to the business and we don't do it."

While no means scientific or complete, it is a good starting place to have a debate among IT, Finance, and the business units of where to spend time, money, and organizational resources in the short and long-terms.

You can divide the numerator by the denominator for a ratio of importance: how "good" we are today versus how much we need it. A ratio of 100% means we're spot on and we've matched our capabilities with our business needs. A low ratio, say 10–20%, might mean we should debate doing this sooner rather than later, and it's probably a priority for our EPM roadmap.

Figure 9.4 shows the aggregate results for the 12 large organizations (revenue > $1 billion) in the sample of 88 attendees (note that more than one person from each organization could submit results, and company numbers were then averaged). Blanks are respondents who chose not to answer.

The five EPM components that scored the lowest, and therefore have the most potential for impact are:

1. Constraints
2. Drivers and targets
3. "The middle" (data relationship management [DRM], etc.)
4. Planning
5. Modeling

A few other interesting observations include the range of company scores went from 49% (company 9) to 107.8% (company 8). Company 8 is "overachieving" in a number of areas including management and statutory consolidation and reporting, self-serve reporting and working with the right metrics, and using facts learned in analytics to feed what-if models. This means they are putting more effort and resources into things that are either already taken care of or don't have as much impact on the business as other areas do. Notice that company 8 is suffering in "the middle"—and probably doesn't have common master data for its plans and all the areas it's overachieving on. I'm guessing that there's a lot of manual effort in that organization spent on managing metadata.

Company 5, which is the example I used for Figure 9.3, has a total "score" of 57.2%—there is certainly much room here for improvement on EPM adoption.

	1	2	3	4	5	6	7	8	9	10	11	12	AVG	RANK
Modeling	14.3%	30.0%	30.0%	50.0%	30.0%	60.0%	133.3%	50.0%	30.0%	100.0%	90.0%	85.7%	58.6%	5
Drivers/Targets	11.1%	33.3%	50.0%	80.0%	55.6%	50.0%	66.7%	40.0%	37.5%	87.5%	80.0%	20.0%	51.0%	2
Constraints	37.5%			70.0%	11.1%	80.0%	80.0%	40.0%	20.0%	100.0%		20.0%	51.0%	1
Planning	80.0%	80.0%	40.0%	40.0%	55.6%	70.0%	37.5%	33.3%	40.0%	66.7%	80.0%	70.0%	57.8%	4
Reforecasting	100.0%	80.0%	80.0%	57.1%	22.2%	70.0%	37.5%	66.7%	85.7%	100.0%	90.0%	200.0%	82.4%	12
Variance	80.0%	80.0%	60.0%	60.0%	80.0%	60.0%	100.0%	66.7%		100.0%	70.0%	77.8%	75.9%	10
Management Consolidation/Report	100.0%	70.0%	80.0%	70.0%	100.0%	85.7%	70.0%	300.0%	50.0%	133.3%	88.9%	80.0%	102.3%	14
Connecting Management/Statutory Consolidation/Report	100.0%	60.0%	80.0%	70.0%	60.0%	100.0%	100.0%	100.0%	37.5%	100.0%	75.0%	75.0%	79.8%	11
Statutory Consolidation/Report	100.0%	80.0%	80.0%	70.0%	150.0%	100.0%	80.0%	300.0%	100.0%	75.0%	100.0%	60.0%	107.9%	15
Drill Down, Slice/Dice	20.0%	100.0%	50.0%	33.3%	60.0%	100.0%	114.3%	10.0%	28.6%	75.0%	77.8%	60.0%	60.7%	7
Self-Serve/Metrics	20.0%	71.4%	60.0%	33.3%	22.2%	100.0%	100.0%	250.0%	37.5%	100.0%	75.0%	22.2%	74.3%	9
Analytics			125.0%	33.3%	77.8%	70.0%	77.8%	33.3%	60.0%	100.0%	70.0%	25.0%	67.2%	8
Fact-Based into Models	83.3%		75.0%	22.2%	100.0%	100.0%	85.7%	250.0%	44.4%	116.7%	60.0%	25.0%	87.5%	13
Predictive Analytics	83.3%		75.0%	22.2%	14.3%	100.0%	57.1%	66.7%	44.4%	125.0%	50.0%	25.0%	60.3%	6
The Middle (Data Relationship Management, Data Warehouse)	80.0%	30.0%	20.0%	80.0%	20.0%	70.0%	100.0%	10.0%	70.0%	70.0%	80.0%	33.3%	55.3%	3
Company Score (AVG)	65.0%	65.0%	65.0%	52.8%	57.2%	81.0%	82.7%	107.8%	49.0%	96.6%	77.6%	58.6%		

Figure 9.4   Aggregate Results of EPM Survey for Large Companies, August 2012

Return on Investment and Total Cost of Ownership

There was a sidebar in an issue of CIO magazine addressing return on investment (ROI) versus total cost of ownership (TCO).[7]

It said ROI quantifies both cost and benefit of projects and TCO includes only costs. In their survey (of 225 technology managers), about 60% said ROI influenced project justification and 40% said TCO helped justify the decision.

I don't think it's one or the other: It's both. The total cost of ownership needs to be included in the cost side of the ROI equation. ROI is "simply" the difference between how much something costs and how much cash it brings in the door (adjusted over time). I say "simply" because the devil is in the details of cost and cash in.

Here are some of the "total" cost ingredients to consider when developing your ROI for EPM:

- Cost to build or acquire the system (hardware, software, network costs)
- Don't forget the ancillary costs to the above (e.g., a system may require an add-on license for a relational database management system [RDBMS] or middleware)
- Cost of capital
- Cost to operate, maintain, and upgrade
- Training costs (administrators and users)
- Cost to install and implement
- Cost to upgrade or troubleshoot and fix any impact the system will have on other existing systems
- Potential consulting cost to reengineer processes that are being automated
- Cost to temporarily back-fill any headcount that has been "seconded" for this initiative
- Labor components of all of the above (procurement staff, IT staff, new-hire administrators, trainers, consultants, and so on)

And here are some of the cash-in-the-door ingredients to consider:

- How many net new customers will we acquire by having the new or updated system that we wouldn't otherwise have, and what's the average lifetime revenue per customer?
- How many more products or services can we sell?
- Will the system let me improve my prices or price/volume mix?
- Will the system make my margin improve . . . measurably?
- Will the system increase the velocity of cash flow?
- Can I improve cross-sell and up-sell opportunities?

And in a subtle twist: Look at less cash out the door:

- Will the system make me more efficient and produce more with fewer resources (measurable productivity)?
- Is there a direct headcount reduction associated with this initiative?
- Can I reduce inventory costs? Raw material costs? Transportation and storage costs?
- Will it reduce my selling, general, and administrative expenses?
- Can it reduce debt and/or improve our cost of capital?

One approach to reduce the reliance on nebulous ROI is to create several layers of IT investments each requiring a different approach to justification. For example:

1. **Infrastructure and "lights on" operations.** This is the fixed cost that it takes to run the business effectively and efficiently. It includes the network infrastructure, servers and desktops, office productivity and messaging software and the staff to administer them. This is the first part of the annual IT budget. ROI may be a known quantity or even a nonissue.
2. **Tactical business systems.** These are your General Ledger (G/L), enterprise resource planning (ERP), time and expense—supply-chain systems that generate, track, and reconcile day-to-day business transactions. This is the second part of the annual IT budget, with some allowance for unexpected CAPEX. ROI is case by case.
3. **Strategic systems.** These are the systems that you may or may not have on your roadmap, but get introduced or accelerated due to competitive pressures. You are convinced that this system (or upgrade) will give you a measurable advantage in the market and will help you outperform your competitors. Sometimes, the ROI will not be quantifiable.

ROI has always been a nebulous tool for justifying IT investments. While an ROI case should be included in making a decision (around upgrading, new systems, training decisions, etc.) it may not be the primary consideration.

Furthermore, EPM can help you get better at estimating and tracking ROI of any project, just run it through the management operating system:

- Model the investment and expected returns, include all the costs in the TCO list.
- Add targets to the right scenario.
- Turn the right scenario into a plan (perhaps include project planning in your Commit cycle).

This is where many organizations have heartburn. Many projects are sold on their potential reduction in headcount, but few are held accountable to those reductions. Putting it in a plan and monitoring the variance holds managers accountable. Some steps to do that include:

- Report on the current spend, gains, and milestones, communicate the variance to all stakeholders.
- Analyze why you got the results you got and find out if you're on course to meet the expectations you modeled or if you need to readjust commitments (on both the cost and benefit sides).
- Get better at doing ROI estimates, accountability, and assessment.
- Call it "Return on Investment Performance Management."

Standard Architecture

If we take all of the enabling technologies presented, add the most common IT enablement or governance capabilities, and put them into one "Information Architecture," it might look like Figure 9.5.

Many of these components are available as cloud services today, more so in the transactional platform area, but cloud services in the EPM space are arriving quickly. Having agreement in IT on this construct allows for the separation of responsibilities into various domains.

Your EPM Roadmap

There are a myriad ways to impact business results using EPM tools and processes. To design the most impactful initiatives, start with company or organizational unit strategic objectives, and then go through the steps outlined and summarized in this checklist:

1. Choose a business impact area (revenue growth, operating margin, cash cycle, asset utilization, etc.).
2. Select the business function(s) that are most accountable (Marketing, Sales, Operations, R&D, Shared Services, Finance, etc.).
3. Identify one or more decision process steps that lack visibility (Gather, Understand, Debate, Commit).
4. Select one or more roles within functions (strategic, operational, tactical execution).
5. Identify the top value drivers/KPIs for that role.
6. Select an EPM process and/or tool that matches the decision process.

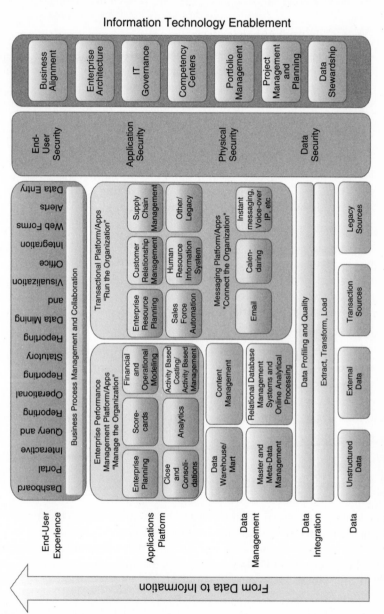

Figure 9.5   Standard EPM Architecture

Your EPM roadmap should address building a foundation to support the four main questions (see the Business Questions section in Chapter 4).

1. What do we want to happen in the business?
   - Financial modeling and scenario planning (e.g., enterprise planning)
   - Strategic Finance (long-range Income Statement, Balance Sheet and Cash-Flow forecasting and modeling)
   - Operational modeling (like activity-based costing [ABC], activity-based management [ABM])
   - Scorecards, strategy maps
2. How do we want it to happen?
   - Enterprise budgeting, planning and forecasting
   - Workforce/resource planning, project planning, CAPEX planning
   - Operational planning (e.g., demand planning)
3. What actually happened in the business?
   - Financial reporting
   - Operational reporting
   - Management reporting
   - Statutory consolidation and reporting
   - Dashboards, scorecards
4. Why did it happen?
   - Financial and operational analytics
   - Profitability analytics
   - Predictive analytics

And then a way to bring the data and relationships together in a meaningful way:

- Master data management
- Data quality management

To develop or refresh your EPM roadmap, think big and start small. Thinking big is done with the management operating system. Starting small is done with all of the initiatives that fit into the management operating system. These steps should help you articulate the business value of EPM and align it to your roadmap:

1. Do the functional value mapping exercise from Chapter 8 and look at the top drivers. Make sure the initiatives address those drivers. For

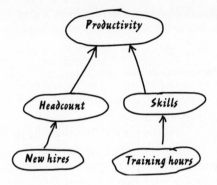

Figure 9.6   Value Chain

example, let's say you document the value chain in your organization and part of it looks like Figure 9.6.

At the top of the chain, the most relevant, material, volatile driver, is productivity.

2. Now we walk productivity through the management operating system:
   - Debate: Productivity model and training investment scenarios
   - Commit: Workforce Plan
   - Gather: Productivity dashboard, by department
   - Analyze: Productivity correlated to number of training hours
   - Middle: Master data management of employee

3. Crosswalk the relevant technologies through each initiative:
   - Productivity model and training investment scenarios: Financial and operational modeling
   - Workforce plan: Operational planning
   - Productivity dashboard, by department: Operational reporting
   - Productivity correlated to number of training hours: Operational analytics
   - Master data management of employee: Data Relationship Management

4. This gives the list of initiatives. Some clients tend to name each initiative and give it an identity in order to discuss it and debate it better:
   1. The do-more model
   2. Workforce planning
   3. Productivity dashboard
   4. Productivity cube
   5. One employee

5. Plot each initiative on two axes: Business Value versus Ease of Implementation.

- Consider your organizational readiness (ease of implementation) to develop and adopt the initiative. Here are some elements to consider:

    - **Time.** Is the need urgent or can it wait? If it can wait, how long: a quarter, a year, two years?
    - **Money.** Can you afford it? Think of the total cost of ownership, and also think of value rather than pure dollars: What's the ROI?
    - **Resources.** Do you have the staff to manage this initiative? Do your users have the bandwidth to participate?
    - **Risk.** Are you willing to take the risk to deploy? Are you willing to take the risk to do nothing?
    - **Culture.** Do you have the executive sponsorship and political will to get it done?

- Business Value = the most material drivers that are most closely connected to strategic objectives.

6. Stratify your initiatives into waves that are achievable. For example, see Figure 9.7 which shows both the plotting of each initiative and the division into waves.

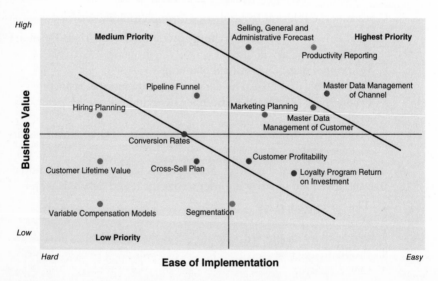

Figure 9.7   Initiatives Organized into Achievable Work Packages

Organizational Readiness: The EPM Center of Excellence

IT, Finance, Operations, and Shared Services all share the same goals of the business while their points of views can differ. IT can focus on standards, solutions, and security, while Finance can focus on the P&L, balance sheet and cash flow, Operations on customer care, and Shared Services on cost improvements. Each of them comes back to, for example:

- Profitable revenue growth
- Operational efficiency
- Asset utilization
- Customer satisfaction
- Product quality

It's this common ground of business results that allow them to come together in a Center of Excellence (sometimes referred to as a Competency Center) and help design, deliver, and support EPM initiatives.

The scope of the EPM Center of Excellence can include:

- Driving out requirements
- Owning the roadmap
- Training users/managers/developers
- Practices and standards for EPM process and tools
- Facilitate change management
- Roles and responsibilities for the management and ownership of EPM and master data
- Visibility, transparency, and access to master data (related properties and hierarchies)
- Communicate governance issues and decisions
- Delivery (solutions, analysis, reporting)

Refer to Chapter 7 of Howard Dresner's book *The Performance Management Revolution* for additional details.[8] The analyst firm Gartner, Inc. has some good information on EPM and BI competency centers as well.

Paralyzed by Feuds?

There may be at least three "management system" camps in your organization: the ERP camp, the data warehouse/BI camp, and the performance management camp. Some are run by IT, some by Finance, and still some by Operations (or key business units [BUs]). Each camp thinks they have the solution to the enterprise information systems strategy, yet each could be contributing to building silos, splitting environments, and wasting resources.

This can be a paralyzing situation when each group starts to compete for senior management attention and funding.

One thing I have found is that these groups have more in common than they think: they all have a concern for master data, for one version of the truth, for ETL, for the end-user experience . . . and for funding. By coming together and determining how they complement each other, they will be able to share infrastructure, resources, and deliverables. They will be able to prioritize their combined portfolio based on the business demands: market share, profitability, cash flow, and so on.

Instead of "duking it out," the three groups must come together and align their missions (and desired outcomes) with each other, and—more importantly—with the strategic objectives of the company as a whole. What does the company demand that they do?

I was recently working with a large division of a Fortune 500 holding company. They have told Wall Street that their three priorities are: cost reduction (to react to a market downturn in their product areas), productivity improvement (to further improve margins), and price changes (to capture additional revenue). Meanwhile, they are embarking on four distinct IT programs: BI, Integration, Shared Services, and CRM. While a case can be made on how each program can have an impact on each corporate priority, no one is looking at how aligning the four initiatives can have even more impact on those priorities.

Our advice, in a nutshell, is to form an EPM advisory group to bring together the teams (IT, Finance, and Operations) and the four initiatives to:

1. Remove any duplication of efforts (especially in ETL)
2. Validate the alignment of each effort to the three strategic priorities
3. Consolidate project plans (including software vendor selection) to get the fastest time to implementation and the most bang for the buck
4. Give the advisory group the authority to review budgets and spends and to perform a "gate review" of each subinitiative

For this to work, they have to pick one senior executive to own EPM. In this case, it's the CFO—still working closely with the CIO—but the buck stops with the CFO. This single point of accountability provides a bias for action and helps alleviate the paralysis.

EPM and Incentive Plans

Executing on your corporate goals depends on the behavior of your people. You want your incentive plans to drive that behavior. You want different behaviors in different parts of the organization (I think of it in eight distinct functions, in three different layers—strategic, operational, and tactical). *And* the drivers of behavior at all 24 of those intersections (eight functions times three layers) *must* align with your corporate objectives.

So for example, some of the key drivers could be:

- Innovation and quality in your products group
- Revenue and forecast accuracy in the sales group
- Inventory and margin in the distribution and supply chains
- Brand awareness in Marketing

These drivers are directly "influence-able" by the people that live in each of those intersections—they are not nebulous, or out of reach like corporate earnings before interest taxes, depreciation, and amortization (EBITDA). Employees want to know they have some control over their variable compensation. Of course, the farther up the chain you are, the more accountability you have for overall earnings.

So while it is more complex to track 24 different "bonus plans," you will get the granular level of detail you need to have all the moving parts working toward the same goals. And there is decent technology for modeling, budgeting, and tracking these plans. EPM is a great way to include those measures and plans in the overall management system of the organization.

When you go through the exercise of discovering what those drivers are at each intersection, you may come up with some new insights that you will want to bonus people on. For example, when I did this exercise for a large beverage company, the new insights were product-line profitability (should we expand or contract brands/containers?) and retail stockouts. Yours could be in the areas of training, campaign effectiveness, or other areas.

As for the percentage contribution, the most common plan is x% for individual goals (management by objectives [MBOs], or tactical metrics), y% for department/function goals, and z% for corporate attainment. As you go higher in the food-chain, your z percentage increases.

Also ask yourself if you have the company culture that would welcome or shun a scorecard that shows where people (roles, actually), departments/functions, and the company are at a given point towards meeting/exceeding goals. It could create some healthy competition (or some resentment!) and eventually, EPM becomes every manager's job.

How Do You Get Started?

If you can see the benefit of bringing together the four strategy-to-execution processes (Debate, Commit, Gather, and Understand) specifically for EPM, and your calculations tell you that there can be a positive ROI, then how do you get started with this new discipline? Follow these seven steps:

1. Enroll the business: Show this framework to your team, to IT, and to your senior management. Help them see a vision for the discipline around managing performance and executing on strategy. I have found that drawing it live on a whiteboard, giving examples along the way and highlighting connections that don't currently exist makes a big difference (bigger than showing the framework as a PowerPoint slide, for example).

2. Find your specific drivers of value that materially affect suppler objectives (like we did in the example for Lenovo in Chapter 7 with cost of goods sold [COGS] and days payable outstanding [DPO]).

3. Map the value chain of those drivers of value right across the organization and down through the layers so your executive management team can see the impact that suppliers have in areas other than production and procurement. This becomes your supplier value map. Also show them how those drivers relate to overall company strategic objectives.

4. Work with your IT team and inventory the current systems (process and technologies) in each area of the framework. Also, understand IT's current roadmap for systems that relate to the value drivers mapped in Step 3.

5. Map the current systems and roadmap systems to the value drivers and focus on the gaps: What are you not measuring, monitoring, analyzing or planning for that drives supplier performance? Also, cut out the noise: Prioritize those outputs (reports, analyses, etc.) that have the greatest impact on the business.

6. Realign the IT roadmap and current systems with those areas that have the most material impact on the value drivers that affect supplier performance. Then begin the project of updating the current initiative or implementing the new initiative.

7. Periodically review the systems and processes with the value map you created earlier to see if you are on track or if course corrections are required.

The enrollment and discovery steps above are necessary to align processes and IT initiatives with supplier strategy and corporate strategy. While going through these steps, companies have found additional side benefits that they weren't expecting. For example, one client in the energy sector uncovered 13 technology-related initiatives being undertaken by different business units and departments that the CIO and his team did not know anything about—each one was duplicating the effort of getting at the data, using a

Table 9.1   How EPM Supports Nature's Rules for Survival

Nature's 10 Rules for Survival	Supported by the Discipline of EPM
1. Diversify across generations.	In the Debate about strategic objectives (especially revenue growth), build financial and operational models that include scenarios for mergers, acquisitions, and divestitures of products; customers; geography; and capabilities. Continue to optimize your models by connecting them to learning done in the Commit process—especially drivers, constraints, and assumptions from budgets, plans and forecasts (and actuals).
2. Adapt to the changing environment, and specialize.	Base your analysis (Understand) on what you learn from Gather (actuals, variances, events) as well as what you created in Debate (e.g., forecast accuracy, actual ROI, and so on). Assign accountability to changes in Commit via enterprise planning (workforce plans, for example).
3. Celebrate transparency. Every species knows which species will eat it and which will not.	When you interconnect all parts of the performance management framework to a common business language, common data, definitions, meta-data, and master data, and you use performance management tools to give visibility to the organization, you create transparency—not just for results, but also for the cause and effect of those results as well as the reasons why you were after those results in the first place (strategic objectives, targets, models, and plans).
4. Plan and execute systematically, not compartmentally. Every part of a plant contributes to its growth.	This whole framework is predicated on systematic planning for the enterprise: financial and operational.
5. Form groups and protect the young. Most animals travel in flocks, gaggles, and prides. Packs offer strength and efficacy.	Packs, or work teams, divisions, strategic business units, projects, and so on, generally live at the intersection of a business function and a layer in the business (strategic, operational, or tactical). Have the performance management framework honor their unique perspectives, yet interconnect with the rest of the organization. Help "protect" the pack with the right HR KPIs.
6. Integrate metrics. Nature brings the right information to the right place at the right time. When a tree needs water, the leaves curl; when there is rain, the curled leaves move more water to the root system.	Measure the right things. Cut out the noise. Focus and align on the most material and volatile drivers of value in the business. Turn the data into actionable information.

(Continued)

Table 9.1   (Continued)

Nature's 10 Rules for Survival	Supported by the Discipline of EPM
7. Improve with each cycle. Evolution is a strategy for long-term survival.	The whole cycle fosters continuous improvement (as in the Commit to Debate example above). Performance management maturity comes by interlinking (in both directions) each component of the framework.
8. Right-size regularly, rather than downsize occasionally. If an organism grows too big to support itself, it collapses; if it withers, it is eaten.	A part of your continuous Debate is around resources (full-time equivalent; property, plant, and equipment, etc.)—what is the optimal level of the workforce, of facilities, of capital, to deliver on our strategic goals? Agree in the Debate and execute via plans in the Commit.
9. Foster longevity, not immediate gratification. Nature does not buy on credit and uses resources only to the level that they can be renewed.	A balance of short-term and long-term targets are required to execute beyond just the quarter.
10. Waste nothing, recycle everything. Some of the greatest opportunities in the 21st century will be turning waste—including inefficiency and underutilization—into profit.	Measures and results around efficiency, productivity, waste, utilization, and so on are all baked in to the performance management cycle. Benchmark yourself internally and externally to see what's normal and give yourself "exceed" scenarios in your forecasts to overachieve.

Adapted from Adam Werbach, "Nature's 10 Simple Rules for Business Survival," *Strategy for Sustainability: A Business Manifesto.* Cambridge, MA: Harvard Business Press, 2009.

variety of front-end tools, and did not include controls or data governance in their projects. The CIO, with the CEO's support, then used the value map as the "North Star" for the entire IT portfolio.

An insurance provider's CFO discovered a plethora of metrics that were being reported monthly for no other reason than "it was easy to get at the data."

When finished with the exercise, one health care CEO declared that the value map (the entire business on one sheet of paper) would be his "accountability" map to make sure all layers of the business were working on executing strategy.

Hopefully, you can use this new framework to bring discipline to your supplier performance management and you will certainly get benefits (known and unknown) from the previous seven steps.

Summary

By now I hope you can see how EPM done right helps facilitate:

- Managing change
- Managing points of view
- Managing the debate
- Managing information
- Managing resources

Ultimately, the management operating system for your organization is not just an EPM process, but also, an overall management discipline that could very well be the foundation of your organization's survival. I'll leave you with this comparison of Nature's 10 Rules for Survival[9] and how it's directly supported by EPM and the management operating system as a discipline (see Table 9.1). And, more than survive, my hope is that you thrive with EPM and be among the most competitive organizations in your industry.

Notes

1. Random House Unabridged Dictionary. New York, New York: Random House Reference, 2nd Revised Edition, 1994.
2. David M. Upton and Bradley R. Staats, "Radically Simple IT," *Harvard Business Review*, March 2008.
3. Robert S. Kaplan and David P. Norton, *Alignment*, Harvard Business School Press, 2006.
4. Peter Drucker, *The Practice of Management*, Harper, 1954.
5. Daniel Pink, *Drive: The Surprising Truth About What Motivates Us*, Riverhead Books, 2011.
6. Bo Burlingham and Jack Stack, *The Great Game of Business: Unlocking the Power and Profitability of Open-Book Management*. New York: Doubleday, 1992.
7. Kim S. Nash, www.cio.com/article/331763/TCO_versus_ROI, retrieved October 23, 2012.
8. Howard Dresner, The *Performance Management Revolution: Business Results Through Insight and Action*. Hoboken, NJ: John Wiley and Sons, 2007.
9. Adam Werbach, *Strategy for Sustainability: A Business Manifesto*. Cambridge, MA: Harvard Business Press, 2009.

APPENDIX: AN EPM MATURITY MODEL

Maturity models are useful tools to help you understand what your capabilities are now and where you want them to be in the future. They are not "the truth" about how things should be, they are useful models to help engage your stakeholders in a debate about your aspirations and roadmap for improving your competence in a given area.

There are several good maturity models related to EPM and business intelligence (BI); for example, those from Gartner, The Data Warehouse Institute (TDWI), and others. Typically they go from an ad hoc or lagging level of maturity to world class. It's useful to peg your organization's current state and to discuss your aspirations. Not all companies want to be world class since there's a cost associated with that.

The EPM Done Right maturity model is based on the management operating system described in this book. At a very high level you could say that the journey to EPM maturity starts with the four corners (Planning, Reporting, Analytics, and Modeling). Once those are relatively mature, the next stage in the journey is the middle: bringing together the four corners and sharing common data, metadata, master data, rules, and so on. And the last leg of the journey would be the arrows, or connections, among each of the cornerstones. This is when EPM becomes an overall management and continuous learning process in the organization. Of course, your journey won't be that sequential nor will it be neat and tidy—there will be missteps, do-overs, and possibly some project failures. And you may focus on one or two cornerstone areas until they are highly mature before venturing out to the complete cycle. However you approach it, this model is a good way to set direction and track progress.

As mentioned, using the management operating system components, the model comprises the cornerstones, the middle, and the connectors, as shown in Figure A.1. I've also added a section for Governance since this is a critical success factor in any EPM project.

As described in Chapter 9, each circle in Figure A.1 gets a score: how well you do the thing divided by how much you need the thing. A current state assessment would measure how well you do the thing now and how much you need the thing now. A desired future state plan would score based on how well you want to be able to do the thing and how much you think you will need it given potential future circumstances. You can use Table A.1 to help

EPM Cycle Survey: In each circle, enter a numerator (top number) of **how well you do the thing** - on a scalw of 1 (don't do it) to 10 (do it very well), and enter a denominator (bottom number) of **how much you need the thing** – on a sclae of 1 (don't need it) to 10 (must have it). E.g., 1/10 means we don't do and we really need it, 8/2 means we're pretty good at it, but don't need it that much.

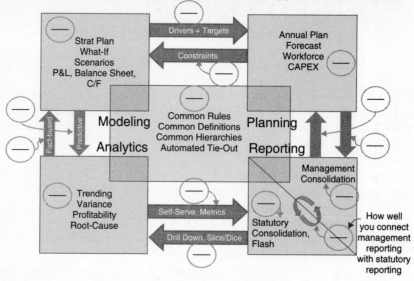

Figure A.1   EPM Maturity Model Scoring Sheet

label your level of maturity. Notice how the connections are within each of the cornerstone columns the more mature the organization.

The scope of each column in Table A.1 can include the following:

Gather includes

- Financial and operational management consolidation and reporting
- Statutory consolidation and reporting
- The bridge between the two (reconciliation)
- Metrics
- Self-serve (interactive reporting)
- Drill down/slice and dice

Understand includes

- Financial and operational analytics
- Uncovering facts to be used in models and decisions
- Predictive analytics

Table A.1 Maturity Model Assessment Components

	Gather	Understand	Debate	Commit	The Middle	Governance
World Class > 90%	Business rules suggest a response/action. On demand delivery of the right information to the right person at the right time.	Big data and predictive analytics covering Customer, Product, and Market domains	Unlimited big-data scenarios Models inform company strategy	Unified enterprise planning, including cash flow, workforce, capital expenditure, and the balance sheet	Global MDM Global standard CoA	Shared Service EPM CoE and corporate governance body. There is a closed loop in the management operating system
Advanced 80–90% total score	Laser focus with drill-paths	Predictive analytics	Models are fed from results and variance	Rolling forecasts	Multiple dimensions are governed (e.g.: Accounts, Product, Customer)	Shared Service EPM CoE and business-unit governance body
Progressive 70% total score	Management by exception with alerting	Guided analytics and self-serve analytics	Long-range strategic financial models with multiple scenarios	Driver-based planning, easy to reforecast	One dimension, usually accounts, is completely governed in MDM to EPM and ERP (and beyond, like CRM)	Center of Excellence for one or more cornerstones (usually starting with Reporting)
Average 40–60% total score	A good balance of financial and operating drivers, leading and lagging indicators	A Revenue and Expense Cube for P&L analytics	Scenarios generated on Spreadsheets. Not shared	Too much detail in plans. Low/no workflow	One or more dimensions is governed by MDM within EPM processes	Audit compliance, still some duplication of effort in reporting and analysis
Lagging < 40% total score	More than five reporting tools, high manual effort	All done in spreadsheets	Finger in the air method	Annual budget done in spreadsheets	Complete silos. High manual effort.	Free for all, low/no controls

Debate includes
- Financial and operational modeling
- Drivers and targets
- Constraints

Commit includes
- Financial and operational planning
- Variance
- Reforecast

The Middle includes
- DRM
- Governance
- Extract, transform, load (ETL)

Governance includes
- Roadmap
- Ownership
- EPM Policies and adherence
- Staffing and organization structure
- Communication and exception processing

You can take the scores from each component of each area and average them (or further weight them) to arrive at an overall column score. See Table A.2 for an example showing scores in Debate.

Table A.2 Sample Maturity Scoring

	How well we do it (x) (Scale of 1–10)	How much we need it (y) (Scale of 1–0)	Score (x/y) × 100
Financial and Operational Modeling	6	8	75
Drivers and Targets	4	10	40
Constraints	1	5	20

You would then take an average of 75, 40, and 20 and score yourself at 45.

An assessment could look like the one in Figure A.2, which attempts to quantify and highlight the gaps.

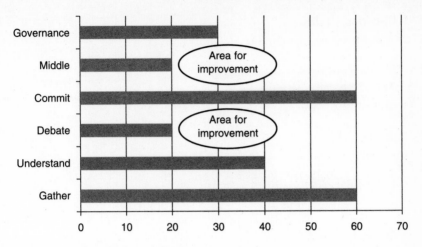

Figure A.2   Example Assessment Score

I would suggest that you tailor this maturity model to your own situation and revise it periodically. Compare it to peers and other EPM organizations you meet at user, industry, and vendor conferences. When you own it and communicate it, all parts of the organization can align to move up the scale to your desired future state.

BIBLIOGRAPHY

Axson, David J. *Best Practices in Planning and Management Reporting: From Data to Decisions*. Hoboken, NJ: John Wiley and Sons, Inc., 2003.

Aziza, Bruno, Joey Fitts, and Jim Bond. *Drive Business Performance: Enabling a Culture of Intelligent Execution*. Hoboken, NJ: John Wiley and Sons, Inc., 2008.

Bardoliwalla, Nenshad, Stephanie Buscemi, and Denise Broady. *Driven to Perform: Risk-Aware Performance Management from Strategy Through Execution*. New York: Evolved Technologist Press, 2009.

The Form of Facts and Figures: Design Patterns for Interactive Information Visualization, Masters Thesis by Christian Behrens, Potsdam University of Applied Science, 2008.

Bogsnes, Bjarte. *Implementing Beyond Budgeting: Unlocking the Performance Potential*. Hoboken, NJ: John Wiley and Sons, Inc., 2009.

Bossidy, Larry, Ram Charan, and Charles Burck. *Execution: The Discipline of Getting Things Done*. New York: Crown Business, 2002.

Bossidy, Larry, and Ram Charan. *Confronting Reality: Doing What Matters to Get Things Right*. New York: Crown Business, 2004.

Broadbent, Marianne, and Ellen Kitzis. *The New CIO Leader: Setting the Agenda and Delivering Results*. Gartner, Inc., 2005.

Brown, John Seely, and Paul Duguid. *The Social Life of Information*. Cambridge, MA: Harvard Business School Press, 2002.

Burlingham, Bo, and Jack Stack. *The Great Game of Business: Unlocking the Power and Profitability of Open-Book Management*. New York: Doubleday, 1992.

Buytendijk, Frank. *Performance Leadership: The Next Practices to Motivate Your People, Align Stakeholders, and Lead Your Industry*. New York: McGraw-Hill, 2008.

Buytendijk, Frank. *Dealing with Dilemmas: Where Business Analytics Fall Short*. Hoboken, NJ: John Wiley and Sons, Inc., 2010.

Capron, Laurence, and Will Mitchell. *Build, Borrow, or Buy: Solving the Growth Dilemma*. Cambridge, MA: Harvard Business Press, 2012.

Stuart K. Card, Jock Mackinlay, Ben Shneiderman (Editors), *Readings in Information Visualization: Using Vision to Think*. San Francisco, CA: Morgan Kaufmann, 1999.

Charan, Ram. *What the CEO Wants You to Know: How Your Company Really Works*. New York: Crown Business, 2001.

Charan, Ram. *What the Customer Wants You to Know: How Everybody Needs to Think Differently About Sales*. New York: Penguin Group, 2007.

Cokins, Gary. *Performance Management: Integrating Strategy, Execution, Methodologies, Risk and Analytics*. Hoboken, NJ: John Wiley and Sons, Inc., 2009.

Collins, Jim. *Good to Great: Why Some Companies Make the Leap . . . and Others Don't*. New York: HarperCollins, 2001.

Collins, Jim, and Jerry Porras. *Built to Last: Successful Habits of Visionary Companies*. New York: HarperCollins, 1997.

Davenport, Tom and Jeanne Harris. *Competing on Analytics: The New Science of Winning*. Cambridge, MA: Harvard Business School, 2007.

De Bono, Edward, *Atlas of Management Thinking*. Pelican, 1983.

de Geus, Arie. *The Living Company*. Longview Publishing, Ltd., 2002.

de Waal, Andre. *Quest for Balance: The Human Element in Performance Management Systems*. Hoboken, NJ: John Wiley and Sons, 2002.

Dresner, Howard. *The Performance Management Revolution: Business Results Through Insight and Action.* Hoboken, NJ: John Wiley and Sons, Inc., 2007.

Dresner, Howard. *Profiles in Performance: Business Intelligence Journeys and the Roadmap for Change.* Hoboken, NJ: John Wiley and Sons, 2009.

Drucker, Peter. *The Practice of Management,* Harper, 1954.

Duggan, William. *Strategic Intuition.* New York: Columbia University Press, 2007.

Drucker, Peter, and Joseph Maciariello. *The Effective Executive in Action: A Journal for Getting the Right Things Done.* New York: HarperCollins, 2005.

Few, Stephen. *Now You See It: Simple Visualization Techniques for Quantitative Analysis.* Oakland, CA: Analytics Press, 2009.

Fraser, Robin, and Jeremy Hope. *Beyond Budgeting: How Managers Can Break Free from the Annual Performance Trap.* Cambridge, MA: Harvard Business School Press, 2003.

Hamel, Gary. *The Future of Management,* Cambridge, MA: Harvard Business School Press, 2007.

Hope, Jeremy. *Reinventing the CFO: How Financial Managers Can Transform Their Roles and Add Greater Value.* Cambridge, MA: Harvard Business School Press, 2006.

Kaplan, Robert S. *The Balanced Scorecard.* Cambridge, MA: Harvard Business School Press, 1996.

Kaplan, Robert S., and David Norton. *Alignment: Using the Balanced Scorecard to Create Corporate Synergies.* Cambridge, MA: Harvard Business School Press, 2006.

Kaplan, Robert S., and David Norton. *Strategy Maps: Converting Intangible Assets into Tangible Outcomes.* Cambridge, MA: Harvard Business School Press, 2004.

Kaplan, Robert S., and David Norton. *The Strategy-Focused Organization: How Balanced Scorecard Companies Thrive in the New Business Environment.* Cambridge, MA: Harvard Business School Press, 2001.

Malone, Thomas. *The Future of Work: How the New Order of Business Will Shape Your Organization, Your Management Style and Your Life.* Cambridge, MA: Harvard Business School Press, 2004.

Mankins, Michael, Steele, Richard. *"Turning Great Strategy Into Great Performance,"* Cambridge, MA: Harvard Business Review, 2005.

Marr, Bernard. *Strategic Performance Management: Leveraging and Measuring your Intangible Value Drivers.* Burlington, MA: Butterworth-Heinemann, 2006.

Marr, Bernard. *The Intelligent Company.* Hoboken, NJ: John Wiley and Sons, Inc., 2010.

McGee, Kenneth G. *Heads Up: How to Anticipate Business Surprises and Seize Opportunities First.* Cambridge, MA: Harvard Business School Press, 2004.

Mintzberg, Henry, et al. *Strategy Safari: A Guided Tour Through the Wilds of Strategic Management.* New York: Free Press, 1998.

Neely, Andy, Chris Adams, and Mike Kennerly. *The Performance Prism: The Scorecard for Measuring and Managing Business Success.* Upper Saddle River, New Jersey: Financial Times Prentice Hall, 2002.

Paladino, Bob. *Five Key Principles of Corporate Performance Management.* Hoboken, NJ: John Wiley and Sons, Inc., 2007.

Paladino, Bob. *Innovative Corporate Performance Management: Five Key Principles to Accelerate Results.* Hoboken, NJ: John Wiley and Sons, Inc., 2011.

Pfeffer, Jeffrey, and Robert Sutton. *Hard Facts, Dangerous Half-Truths and Total Nonsense: Profiting From Evidence-Based Management.* Cambridge, MA: Harvard Business School Press, 2006.

Pfeffer, Jeffrey, and Robert Sutton. *The Knowing–Doing Gap: How Smart Companies Turn Knowledge into Action.* Cambridge, MA: Harvard Business School Press, 2000.

Pink, Daniel. *Drive: The Surprising Truth About What Motivates Us,* Riverhead Books, 2011.

Porter, Michael. *Competitive Advantage: Creating and Sustaining Superior Performance*. New York: The Free Press, 1985.

Porter, Michael. *Competitive Strategy: Techniques for Analyzing Industries and Competitors*. New York: The Free Press, 1980.

Ranadive, Vivek. *The Power to Predict: How Real Time Businesses Anticipate Customer Needs, Create Opportunities, and Beat the Competition*. New York: McGraw-Hill, 2006.

Rodek, Jeff, and Kathi Fox. *On the Up and Up*. Sunnyvale CA: Hyperion, 2004.

Schoemaker, Paul, and Robert Gunther. *Profiting from Uncertainty: Strategies for Succeeding No Matter What the Future Brings*. New York: Free Press, 2002.

Schwartz, Peter. *The Art of the Long View: Planning for the Future in an Uncertain World*. New York, New York: Currency Doubleday; Reprint edition, 1996.

Senge, Peter. *The Fifth Discipline: The Art & Practice of The Learning Organization*. Doubleday, 1990.

Shapiro, Carl, and Hal Varian. *Information Rules: A Strategic Guide to the Network Economy*. Cambridge, MA: Harvard Business School Press, 1998.

Stiffler, Mark. *Performance: Creating the Performance-Driven Organization*. Hoboken, NJ: John Wiley and Sons, Inc., 2006.

Tapscott, Don, and David Ticoll. *The Naked Corporation: How the Age of Transparency Will Revolutionize Business*. New York: Free Press, 2003.

Tufte, Edward. *The Visual Display of Quantitative Information*. Cheshire, CT: Graphics Press, 2001.

Werbach, Adam. *Strategy for Sustainability: A Business Manifesto*. Cambridge, MA: Harvard Business Press, 2009.

Zaffron, Steve, and Dave Logan. *The Three Laws of Performancen Rewriting the Future of Your Organization and Your Life (J-B Warren Bennis Series)*. New York: Jossey-Bass, 2009.

ABOUT THE AUTHOR

For over thirty years Ron has been involved in Finance Systems and Processes, from his first job at Deloitte, Haskins + Sells as a 19-year-old programmer writing the Journal Entry subsystem for a trial balance program, through Lotus 1-2-3, Accpac (now Sage), and custom-developed systems (like BOX, the Broker of Obligations and Transactions that connected US Navy accounting systems with Citibank purchase cards), to nine years at Hyperion Solutions (later acquired by Oracle) where he helped raise the toddler now called Enterprise Performance Management. Today, Ron helps organizations understand and realize the business benefits of EPM processes and technologies.

Always focused on making tangible contributions to his clients, Ron consults with passion, integrity, and transparency. Originally from Toronto, Canada, his furniture is in Northern Virginia.

INDEX